FAT GAY MEN

INTERSECTIONS
Transdisciplinary Perspectives on Genders and Sexualities
General Editors: Michael Kimmel and Suzanna Walters

Fat Gay Men

Girth, Mirth, and the Politics of Stigma

Jason Whitesel

NEW YORK UNIVERSITY PRESS

New York and London

NEW YORK UNIVERSITY PRESS
New York and London
www.nyupress.org

© 2014 by New York University
All rights reserved

References to Internet websites (URLs) were accurate at the time of writing. Neither the author nor New York University Press is responsible for URLs that may have expired or changed since the manuscript was prepared.

ISBN: 978-0-8147-0838-5 (hardback)
ISBN: 978-0-8147-2412-5 (paperback)

For Library of Congress Cataloging-in-Publication data, please contact the Library of Congress.

New York University Press books are printed on acid-free paper,
and their binding materials are chosen for strength and durability.
We strive to use environmentally responsible suppliers and materials
to the greatest extent possible in publishing our books.

Manufactured in the United States of America

c 10 9 8 7 6 5 4 3 2 1
p 10 9 8 7 6 5 4 3 2 1

Also available as an ebook

CONTENTS

ACKNOWLEDGMENTS

I am deeply indebted to all of the Girth & Mirthers whom I met along my research journey. They gave generously of their time for interviews and shepherded me through the ins and outs of the organization. To the Girth & Mirthers—the "Big Eats" bunch, my travel companions to Oklahoma City, especially my roomie at the motel, and my monthly Friday lunch date and travel companion to Convergence—I owe a great deal. They included me, someone who suffers a little from "group" anxiety, in their group and made me feel at home. They even opened up their doors to me beyond the club, making my research experience a delight. I hope I have done them justice in these pages. As one Girth & Mirther aptly pointed out, maybe the story of our collaboration will result in greater visibility for this wonderful organization.

Over the years it took me to complete this book, I had the perfect trifecta of intellectual mentors. Amy Shuman's guidance was invaluable. She deserves a great deal of credit for many of the analytical ideas in this book and for persuading me to refine them. She has extraordinary intellectual breadth and an eye for the big ideas in seemingly unimportant events, the smallest moments, and rituals of everyday life. She understands my work even better than I do and knows what I am up to on every page, and in each passage. Townsand Price-Spratlen, my academic guardian angel, served as the sounding board for my developing ideas. Steve Lopez played a critical role in helping me clarify and organize my thoughts through his tough, constructive criticism. I also want to thank my former graduate student colleagues in the Ohio State University (OSU) Department of Sociology and the Center for Folklore Studies.

Müge Galin was a writer's best friend and provided generous hands-on editorial advice. Her encouragement and her home as a writing sanctuary were sustaining forces throughout the course of revising the manuscript. An amazingly talented and genuinely wonderful person to work with, she helped me serve as a mouthpiece for Girth & Mirth and in the process she herself became a champion for the Girth & Mirthers. I learned a great deal from Müge that improved my book, and I could never have finished it without her.

I gained much from my talks with Peter Hennen, who is an expert in the world of the Bears. I am grateful to him for sharing his expertise on this narrower domain. The vast network of fat studies scholars gave me a forum to share my ideas and brought me up to speed on a more radical view of *fat*'s not being the "four-letter word" our sizist society has made it. I especially want to thank among these scholars Esther Rothblum, Lee Monaghan, Ariane Prohaska, Stefanie Snider, Michaela Null, Marilyn Wann, and Lesleigh Owens for their comments on earlier presentations and drafts of my work, for inviting me to sit on panels, and for participating in some of the conference panels I organized. I also want to extend my gratitude to Susan Alexander, who helped me feel at home in the academy with my particular research interest. She encouraged me to share my work in its various stages in her conference sessions and undergraduate classrooms.

While living in Florida, I could not have asked for a group of more supportive colleagues than those I found at Seminole State College. The faculty in the Social Science Department and my second-floor hallway colleagues were generous sources of strength. I want to thank especially Kerri, Scott, Michael, Patrick, Katie, and Monica. Katie Steinhaus encouraged me to share my work with her humanities undergrads. Monica Butler boosted my self-confidence in my academic potential and gave honest, helpful feedback to me on some of the passages I shared with her.

My research was made possible by several different grants: a Social Justice Research Grant from Coca-Cola and OSU's Multicultural Center, an OSU Sociology departmental award for human rights research, and conference travel grants from the Popular Culture Association/American Culture Association and the American Folklore Society. Through these monies, I was also able to procure the services of Ben Stout and Greg Matthews for their careful transcription assistance.

I want to express my appreciation to the faculty, staff, and graduate students at the Criminal Justice Research Center at Ohio State, who commiserated with me throughout my research and writing years. I appreciate the kind support Ruth Peterson and Laurie Krivo continue to give me as a junior scholar. After I moved to Florida, Ruth helped me get back to Ohio by selecting me to be a fellow of the Crime and Justice Summer Research Institute funded by the National Science Foundation, for which I am deeply grateful. Thus, for a month in the summer of 2011, I was able to work on revisions unencumbered by life's usual distractions, plus I could seek the help of my old support network. During the summer institute, Laurie pushed me to rewrite the opening chapters to identify clearly the heart of the ethnographic story I wanted to tell. I also received helpful feedback from fellow participants at the summer institute and at the Racial Democracy, Crime, and Justice Network conference. It was Ruth and Laurie who introduced me to Ilene, one of the acquisitions editors at New York University Press. I am grateful to the following people at NYUP for their support and enthusiasm for my book: executive editor Ilene Kalish; assistant editor Caelyn Cobb; managing editor Dorothea Stillman Halliday; copy editor Eric Newman; former editorial assistant Aiden Amos; and the series editors, Michael Kimmel and Suzanna Walters. I also thank the anonymous peer reviewers for NYUP who gave me valuable feedback.

During my long journey from project proposal to this book, I appreciated my long walks and talks with Amanda Kennedy, both in person and on the phone. She helped me work out ideas and gain confidence, and she was my go-to person for decompressing and professional release. She always listened to my repeat performances of why I was incapable of writing something or other, and she always let me off easy whenever I became my own worst critic. I am equally indebted to Wade Moore, my partner-in-crime on the gay scene during the years I spent in Ohio. He also became a "poor man's" accountant for me, keeping me out of financial trouble while I was in graduate school. Finally, I don't even know how to begin to acknowledge the loving support of my steadfast partner, Brian Sayers. He suffered alongside me, the struggling academic; he gave me the freedom to disappear for long spells so I could do my writing and he held down the fort so I had a home to come back to.

Introduction

An Ethnographer among Girth & Mirthers

The coffee shop's sidewalk seating area is packed with big gay men who weigh 225 to 350 pounds or more. A large man texts his boy toy on the phone and shares naughty messages with the rest of the group. Beside him, a couple of "big men," as those gathered are wont to call gay men of size, scan the personals on their laptops while a few interested parties look over their shoulders, point, and suggest what profiles to look at next. The younger contingent sits off to the side, some reading tarot cards, others discussing comic books. An older couple talks about their horse out in the country, while keeping an eye on their Blue Great Dane. One big man, a chubby vegetarian with a wizardlike beard, is an animal lover and pulls biscuits from his pocket to give to dogs that walk by with their owners. Later, his partner, the adventurer, shares with me photos he took in Australia. Several vent about work; others talk about movies or celebrity gossip, frustrations with their workout routines, parenting travails, and church; one couple reminisces about their wedding day.

According to one group member, these big men have commandeered the coffee house for tonight, as they do every Friday night, for their own private clubhouse: "It's our coffee shop when we're here." Many have come to this kaffeeklatsch because it "provides an opportunity to get out of the house on Friday nights." This is their haven. They "look forward to it all week." As one member put it, "for a $2 cup of coffee, I can spend five hours laughing and having a ball. It's a chance to unwind from the stresses of the week." Gatherings like this are an opportunity for gay big men simply to get together publicly and have what they consider to be a "normal" social life.

Although some may regard these big men as "deviant" because of their size and gay practices, the foregoing scene describes one of their more ordinary events, though the big men engage in more lewd and bawdy displays as well. Nonetheless, the seemingly innocuous kaffeeklatsch is an achievement for the big men, who have found a place where they feel at home. A public gathering like this might come across as a statement of resistance by a group of big men who take up a lot of space, even the entire coffee house. For the group, however, it is more often a claim to be ordinary in a world that sometimes regards them as misfits. These men, who allowed me a privileged look into their group, are members of an Ohio chapter of an international association called "Girth & Mirth" that provides a social support network for big gay men and their relatively few admirers.

Entering the Big Gay Men's World

Big gay men incur social wounds produced by the stigmas of their size and sexuality combined. As looks are one of the organizing features of the gay world, gay big men have an added exclusion that has not been fully explored. There is the exclusion all gay people experience—a group of people who want equality. Then there is the within-group prejudice big men experience because of their ample size. Gay big men are thus marginalized both for their sexual orientation in a heteronormative society and for their size in gay society, thereby constituting a subaltern within the subaltern. Given their doubly marginal position, they strive for dignity and respect.

How do gay big men respond to the injuries—shaming, desexualization, exclusion, and marginalization—they experience within mainstream and especially in gay society? From the start, what drew me to the Girth & Mirthers, self-described as a club for big gay men, was their refreshing take on "obesity" and the way they creatively and playfully reconfigure the stigma of being fat. That is, they demedicalize being fat and provide a counternarrative to it. This theme underlies everything they say and do and in turn underlies all of my arguments in this book. Constructed to provide a safe space for big men who feel stigmatized, the Girth & Mirth culture has a double appeal for members: It brings out big gay men and engages them in normalizing activities and commensality rituals wherein they can receive friendship in a normal way; it also allows them opportunities to resist stigmatization by playing up their sexual identity through campy behavior and carnival.[1]

In their desire for gay citizenship, Girth & Mirthers engage in a dialogue about ways in which body fascism—the narrow dictates of appearance—warrants reconfiguring, even if it is not always so liberatory. They respond to the shame of fat stigma by playfully disregarding it. As a multiply marginalized group, they use play, sexual display, and eating occasions to achieve a semblance of comfort and carve out a social life for themselves. Their mission is not a fat revolution but a healthy response to oppression. The big men attempt to construct livable and satisfying lives, refusing to be taken out of the running and wanting a fighting chance at being sexually desirable and accepted in gay society. Sometimes they choose an oppositional way of dealing with conformity, using outrageousness and excess as their weapons. Still, they provide an alternative version of gay society that deserves attention.

The Study

For nearly three years, I spent a great deal of time with members of Girth & Mirth. I interacted with them at bar nights, kaffeeklatsches, restaurant outings, pot-luck dinners, holiday bashes, pool parties, game and movie nights, and weekend retreats. The retreats took me outside of the local scene to regional and national events held in the Southwest and Midwest.

While I go into further discussion in the Methodological Appendix of the study participants and how I collected my data, here I would like to briefly remark on my researcher position. During my time in the local group, I was open with members about my researcher status. I told them of my interest in studying the group and identified myself as a gay man and as an enthusiast of the organization. I was a dues-paying member, active in the club, and served functional roles for the group such as selling Jell-O shots and working the door during charity bar nights. The latter task involved checking IDs and handling cover charges, what some members called being a "door whore." Because studying the activities meant I had to participate in them, I always created a total written reconstruction of the night's events at the end of each day. The advantage was that lending a hand at an understaffed event allowed me the opportunity to get to know the men well. The proceeds from my and other volunteers' work went to a local group that provided meals to people living with HIV/AIDS and to a gender and sexuality center for youth.

In retrospect, I think my role at one of the extralocal events called the "Super Weekend," which I describe in chapter 3, was even more compromised than I considered it to be at the time. I was always forthright with my companions, individuals from the local group, who served as "culture-brokers" or intermediaries and whom I consulted to determine how to present myself at the national events. My comrades recommended I attend the Super Weekend as just another member of the local club, which I did, as I came to recognize that explicitly stating my researcher position at the Super Weekend would likely interfere with my interactions with the Girth & Mirthers. Thus, while all of the local Girth & Mirthers who attended the same weekend knew about my research project, most of the other guests did not and assumed I was there with "my club" to have a good time, just as they were.

This decision to withhold my identity, however, led me to experience role strain with regard to which code I should follow: that of the Super Weekenders or that of the researcher. I did not want to assume that transparency was the modus operandi. I understood that a certain amount of masking of identity is tolerated in this context and did not feel that my withholding of information about why I was there was any greater form of exploitation. I was more concerned with how to be as unobtrusive as possible than I was about the ethical compromise of being an observer as well as a participant. I imagine my decision will raise ethical concerns for readers trained in feminist methodologies, as it does for me. My hope is that this "confessional tale" will contribute to the larger literature about appreciating the fruits and perils of making moment-by-moment decisions while being a participant observer.[2]

In order to protect the privacy of those who contributed to my research, I replaced proper names with pseudonyms in most cases, nicknames in some, though entities like the name of the club, Girth & Mirth, I kept as such, as this is the name of the organization worldwide. The group writ large regards itself as a public entity (they enroll in the Pride parades, for example, with the name of the group). As Girth & Mirth is an already public nonprofit social organization, I wanted to acknowledge it as such, allowing the group to gain greater visibility. In various endnotes, I discuss in more length how I changed certain details to preserve anonymity as best I could without losing context.

As a fieldworker who came alone to Girth & Mirth events, I appeared to occupy the status of a chubby-chaser: a slim-build devotee of gay men of size.[3] As the owner of the bar put it, I was "the club's little admirer." My own personal hangups notwithstanding, I am thin, and I continue to gain greater appreciation for the appearance-based privileges that come with my body size. My researcher position as both a partial insider as a gay man, and as an outsider, given my thin privilege, allows me to offer a critique of looksism in the gay world. In many ways, I recognize that Girth & Mirth members look for the same opportunities and respect given to men with idealized body types in the gay community. Indeed, I am an admirer of their cause.

Overview

My examination of the full range of the Girth & Mirthers' activities, from the most ordinary of cultural practices like gatherings at a sidewalk café to the more over-the-top and campy sexualized events, provides a lens for understanding how gay big men cope with stigma by engaging in playful identity reconstruction. In reflecting on the big men's responses to and coping strategies for their doubly marginal position, I lend legitimacy to the ordinary culture of big gay men. I extend what we know about the subjective experience of being fat, the interactional nature of suffering, and the human behavioral responses to size discrimination within the gay community.

In the following chapters, I build on fat studies, disability studies, performance analyses of sexualities, and research on stigmatized social groups to examine the social injuries gay big men incur and their responses to those injuries. My approach departs from existing research in its examination of play as politics. I stretch Erving Goffman's concept of stigma by adding to it Michael Chemers's staging stigma, Chong-Suk Han's defensive stigma management strategies, Marcia Millman's obesity and desexualization, Mikhail Bakhtin's carnivalesque folk culture, Susan Sontag's notes on camp, Gregory Bateson's concept of play, Eve Sedgwick's shame and performativity, and Kathleen LeBesco's politics of performing fatness, all of which is elaborated in this book's Theoretical Appendix. I then use these perspectives to analyze how Girth & Mirthers transform the stigma of being big and gay.

To describe what kind of group Girth & Mirth is, chapter 1 reviews the historical background of the organization, although this history is not sufficient to understand the multiple roles the group plays in the lives of the big men and how it serves to manage their social injuries. This chapter also recounts how some of the members made their initial contact with Girth & Mirth. Finally, it explores some of the collective identities Girth & Mirth assumes: as a social-sexual club, a dining club, a personal-political group, a normalizing group, or a group with "wounded attachments" to the gay community.[4]

Chapter 2 characterizes the social injuries gay big men experience because of their "failure" to be height-weight proportionate, a matter that gets exacerbated in the body-conscious gay community. It sets up the scenario of what it must be like to have to cope daily with the social stigma of being both big and gay. Chapter 3 describes a Pan–Girth & Mirth reunion called the "Super Weekend," held at a gay motel in Oklahoma, where big men redefine themselves as sex objects to remedy the desexualization they commonly experience. This reunion is compared with the big men's Labor Day Convergence described in chapter 4, which explores why people so dispossessed are compelled to be middle-class consumers or long to become sex objects. Taking place in a mainstream luxury hotel, Convergence consists of seminars, a dance, sightseeing, and outings to museums, all of which are about gay big men's seeking class validation and respectability à la Pierre Bourdieu's theory of class distinction. Chapter 5 focuses on alternatives that big men employ to reconfigure shame other than the sexual objectification described in chapter 3 and the class consciousness described in chapter 4. One of these reconfigurations discussed in depth is the big men's joyful disregard of shame, which remains true to the club's moniker, "Girth & Mirth," reflecting its mission. The chapter teases out the possibilities for responding to fat oppression in ways that promote inclusion and healthy acceptance of difference, rather than create or reproduce new hierarchies of marginalization. It identifies the positive and fun-loving strategies that members of Girth & Mirth use to reposition their shame. The Conclusion offers some additional statements on moving beyond stigma management.

1

Coming Together

Post-Stonewall, diversity within the U.S. urban gay community became apparent. This led to the formation of groups such as leathermen, associations for older gay men, and, most relevant to this discussion, the chub/chaser subculture.[1] Girth & Mirth was organized in the 1970s as a national social movement in response to weight discrimination in the gay community, with activities designed to transform big gay men's experiences with shame.[2] The organization was founded by Dick Bernolt and Charlie Brown, a big man and his thin admirer, respectively. It was Brown who took out an ad in the alternative newspaper *The Berkeley Barb*, inviting interested parties.[3] Eventually, the first two Girth & Mirth clubs were started in San Francisco and New York.[4] Then, by 1985, the Affiliated Bigmen's Clubs (ABC) was formed in Seattle to coordinate Girth & Mirth clubs at the national level. In turn, ABC led to an annual Labor Day Convergence.[5] Within the next two decades, national events like Convergence, which originally started with about 100 people, had grown to anywhere from 300 to 1,000 guests, depending on the year.[6] Regionally, smaller Convergences also cropped up. Today, some go through ABC to avoid scheduling conflicts, while others remain rogue events.

The first mention of the Girth & Mirth subculture in mainstream media was in the 1975 play *The Ritz* by Terrence McNally.[7] I learned this from a local Girth & Mirther one night at the hamburger joint Red Robin during the group's monthly "Big Eats," as insiders have coined their dinner outings. This member told me that when he was in a Scottish Catholic high school, he grew tired of being in their dramas and musicals. During his senior year, the musical was *Brigadoon*. With his parents' permission, he instead went outside the school to pursue a part in *The Ritz*, in which he was cast in the role of the chubby-chaser. The folks at the Catholic school were not pleased. In this farce, a fat Cleveland businessman runs away to Manhattan in search of a hiding place from his mobster brother-in-law and unsuspectingly checks into a gay hotel. There, an overzealous chubby-chaser stalks him, literally chasing him around the bathhouse. Thus, we get the first popular reference to the terms *chub* and *chaser* and the subculture to which they belong.[8]

Like many social movements with a collective identity, media and later virtual realities made it easier for subcultures to organize globally. The big men's community was organized around publications, and later around Internet communities. Magazines like *Bulk Male* emerged in the 1970s through the 1990s. This is also where big men's personals ads appeared. By the late 1990s, personals as well as the magazines that used to feature them had moved to the Internet. Websites began to emerge for big men, such as Chubnet and, later, BiggerCity, and personals ads in turn went online and communication became more interactive via chatrooms.[9] The limited research on the now international culture of Girth & Mirth focuses on these media and virtual representations as well as on chaser odysseys, rather than chronicle the immediate and direct personal experiences of big men.[10]

Becoming a Girth & Mirther

According to a longstanding theoretical paradigm in sociology, symbolic interactionism, people sometimes foray into a subculture in response to feeling relegated to the margins, which is indeed the case in big men's seeking out companionship at Girth & Mirth. Clubs worldwide offer a friendship circle to draw big gay men out of social isolation. In this chapter, I chronicle narratives of how big men become Girth & Mirthers, and I explore the club's identity and mission. In response to my question as to what brought them to the club, some said they came for the first time after reading about the club online or in the gay paper or upon the insistence of a friend. Many of them shared with me stories of how they almost gave up on finding happiness as gay big men before they encountered the safe space of Girth & Mirth.

Following Pride Weekend, one member posted on the group's listserv his testimonial. In it, he expressed his deep gratitude to Girth & Mirthers for providing him with a family.

I didn't come out of the closet until the tender age of thirty-seven. When I met my husband, I was over the whole "gay scene." I figured I had my kids, my family, my life (however miserable it was), and could live that way the rest of my life. I didn't need no stinkin' man! But, I met someone different, someone who showed me life isn't all that bad and someone who has the uncanny ability to see the silver lining in everything. So, as you all know, I married him! He was the one that brought me to Girth & Mirth and I have to say he was right when he said, "They are a wonderful bunch of guys and I think you'll like them." I do! I'm very blessed to have met each and every one of you. I'm blessed to have turned the corner instead of becoming a bitter queen! For that, I thank my wittle bald man (my love, my life, my support system) and you guys! You showed me that all gay men are not alike. I'll be forever grateful to you. Happy Pride everyone! Enjoy the rest of Pride month and thanks! See you Friday night at coffee!

Another Girth & Mirther relayed his story of how he got involved in the group the very day he learned he was HIV-positive. As he told me in his interview, his friend ran an intervention and took him to Girth

& Mirth. His introduction to the club came in the nick of time when he may have socially isolated himself.

> The day I found out I was positive, my friend and I were going out for dinner that evening, and I sat down and talked with him that night because I was freaked out. I completely forgot he was coming over, and he showed up and I wasn't ready. He's like, "Dude, we gotta get you outta the house." He said, "I know you're not in the mood for socialization, I know you're not in the mood to be in public, but you know what, think about this problem another day. Get the hell out of the house." He forced my hand. And he took me to Girth & Mirth that night. Before that, I didn't even know they existed.

Yet another man told me he came across an ad for Girth & Mirth when he was looking for a suicide hotline number. As an artist, he worked alone, and when his relationship of eleven years ended, he found himself at a loss. He was suffering from the social injuries inflicted on him as a big gay man, and he finally found the kind of support he needed when he came to join Girth & Mirth. In the interview, he told the following story:

> I had no friends. I was eleven years older, I wasn't in the same physical shape, I was a little bigger—the gray hair and all that stuff. And I kind of felt, I have to get out and I have to socialize or I'm gonna go insane. And quite frankly, I was having suicidal thoughts. I mean, it got bad—because I thought no one would ever even want to speak to me. That's how the bars work. You've gotta be thin and have the right clothes and have the right hair and the whole thing. And I was reading one of these gay newspapers, and looking for some kind of support group for suicide prevention, and came across Girth & Mirth, and thought, "What the hell is that?" So, I called and talked to somebody and thought, "Well, maybe I'll look into that!" And I'm certainly glad I did. It saved my life, quite frankly. Absolutely, I would have, I would have done it.

The three foregoing narratives share the sense of fictive kin that Girth & Mirth offers these big men. Each relays a transitional point when the men were finally able to enjoy a sense of belonging. Such stories have become part of the repertoire of origin stories for many Girth & Mirthers; for the members, they are as important as the historical accounts of the founding of the group.

A Social-Sexual Club

The Ohio chapter of Girth & Mirth is a social club; elsewhere, some chapters are also sexual clubs. Locally, the club has to do with the role of the ordinary—ordinary people attending ordinary events like a pot-luck dinner with friends. It is a place where big men can be friendly and can receive friendship in a normal way, without the hassle of preachy weight-loss sermons.[11] As one member admitted, he simply goes "to make friends and to hang out with other big men from time to time, instead of being at home all the time." Another Girth & Mirther remarked on members' unconditional acceptance of gay men of all sizes.

> It gives people the opportunity to socialize in a way in which they don't have to worry about being chastised or looked down upon because of their size. So there's that format; it's set up so people are expected to be nonjudgmental—it's in its own way more friendly than we see with a lot of other gay groups. One can relate to people that are the same and appreciate people the way they are. Gay men of size are generally one of the most ostracized groups out there, so we provide an environment where we don't allow that to happen.

It became clear from my observations and interviews that Girth & Mirth is about both male companionship and sexuality. One member compared the group to the Centurions, a leather/Levi club, which, according to him, is "wilder." He said, "I hung out with them a lot, at a time when I myself was a little bit wilder." The same man went on to then contrast Girth & Mirth with a Catholic gay men's group in Texas that was, in his words, "almost as if folks were sitting around in a circle apologizing to each other for being gay. It was all about trying to reconcile your sexuality with your spirituality." This is indeed a far cry from what Girth & Mirth is all about: It is *neither* about apologizing for your sexuality *nor* about having to apologize for your size.[12] This man went on to add, "There were certainly a lot of people at the Catholic gay men's support group who weren't terribly far along with this reconciliation." Some Girth & Mirthers will likewise confess that they too are not that far along in terms of making peace with their size and sexuality.

Others grapple with the choices offered to them that may go beyond their comfort level, like the sexual tourism that takes place extralocally at big men's national reunions, such as Convergence or the Super Weekend. However, in response to the needs of most of its members, Girth & Mirth prefers to identify itself as a social club or a family, rather than as a gay group interested in creating sexual opportunities. The following comments of one Girth & Mirther express his wish for the ordinary possibility of simply getting together with friends.

> One of the things I pride myself on with this club is, it's not about sex. It's about camaraderie. It's actually about friendship. It's not about who can screw who first. It's more about people getting together and enjoying each other's company, talking about their week, enjoying each other's lives, and the bad things; and so, when I first joined, I was impressed it wasn't about having sex. It was about actually being with a group of people who like to get together and actually *do* things together. And if somebody is having a hard time or going through trouble, the group definitely provides support. The way they have reached out to folks who've been going through a rough patch I think is just wonderful.

This club member was not alone in his sentiments that the group primarily serves a social, rather than a sexual, function. Members of Girth & Mirth see their roles as being no different from those of any family member who would do anything to help a relative. Local events provide club members with a sense of comfort, in contrast to their experience of exclusion and humiliation in other public settings. Congregation and shared experiences take place in the supportive and nurturing environment the club provides.

A Dining Club

Girth & Mirth can also be characterized as a dining club, where members like to get together to eat, overcoming the social isolation of being fat. Members congregate to create a cultural comfort zone, surrounded as they are by those with similar physical attributes (both in public and private settings) to counter their embarrassment of eating in public and the exclusions that doing so might bring.[13] However, food consumption among Girth & Mirthers is not necessarily the focus of this book, in part to avoid perpetuating the stereotype of fat people sitting around and eating all the time. In fact, as I got to know them, the Girth & Mirthers were about so much more than that. This was brought home when the manager at the bar where the group had its charity night suggested that Girth & Mirth have a hot wings–eating competition or a beer-chugging contest. Some members rejected this suggestion because they thought it would send the wrong message. One member, proposing they instead do a game show night based on the television program "Identity," commented that this would "show we're not just fat guys who eat. We've done things and lived some life." In suggesting this particular game show, this board member wanted to declare that fat gay men in fact constitute a diverse group.

It is important to consider the public/private dimensions of the big men's engagements in and withdrawals from society. As an outsider in my thin privilege, it took me a while to see that big men's making the effort to go out to eat together as a group is a remarkably courageous act.[14] Millman writes about fat people's relationship to food in her chapter "Set Apart: The Fat Person as an Antisocial Figure."[15] In it, she describes how "normal" people can freely go out to eat together, but for fat people, eating out is publicly indicted as "deviant." Therefore they may end up eating at home and, some of them, alone. Thus, they often come to embody the stereotype of the fat person who sneaks around raiding the refrigerator late at night. Girth & Mirth offers an alternative. As one member said of a weekend Convergence, "You can go there, be yourself, pick up talking with people like it was ol' times, and eat in front of people without worrying what someone will think—it's a comfortable environment." Hence, "those who eat and drink together are by this very act tied to one another by a bond of friendship and mutual obligation."[16] This is why members appreciate Girth & Mirth: It allows them to be together and not feel excluded from taking meals with one another in public.

In Girth & Mirth, "the sharing of meals is reciprocal, and there is . . . an exchange of food which constitutes the confirmation of a bond."[17] One member decided that out of the litany of groups he had tried, Girth & Mirth came closest to the Denton Dining Queens—a monthly pot-luck group for gay faculty at the University of North Texas. He said that like the Denton Dining Queens, Girth & Mirthers "are not necessarily about apologizing for your size; nor do they put you on the spot sexually. No sex, no agendas, just getting together and having wonderful dinners."

The Girth & Mirthers hold pot-lucks that are no different from what one would see at a church social. On the group's listserv, the president of the local Girth & Mirth reported on the honor-your-mother pot-luck he attended:

There were twenty-eight who attended the pot-luck at our apartment complex party room. Twenty-eight! We sat inside at the dining tables, we used the coffee and end tables, we sat outside at the picnic tables (with a lovely view of the drained swimming pool), we were everywhere! And the food! Oh my gosh, it was a total gastronomic orgasmic event! Honoring our moms by bringing her favorite dish was a great theme. The salads, casseroles, fried chicken, side dishes, and desserts were so tasty! I wonder just how many quarts of that Paula Deen banana pudding were in that serving dish. Not a drip-drab morsel of a leftover for that one![18]

Clearly, food plays a significant role in Girth & Mirth's community formation. As members of a stigmatized and outcast group, the big men are able to use eating together as an affirmation of intimacy.[19] Georg Simmel observes that eating is an individual need, while partaking of a meal fulfills a social function. The latter transcends the individual by bringing groups together to socialize and form communities, thereby rendering a seemingly ordinary activity like eating a shared experience.[20] Eating is thus a social marker that both unites members and separates Girth & Mirthers from other gay groups—when they have a pot-luck among their friends, they may still be inadvertently withdrawing from the larger society. Subsequent chapters in this book will explore the range of cultural play and social rituals Girth & Mirthers have developed, food being just one of them.

A Personal-Political Group

Girth & Mirth gives us an opportunity to look beyond what we traditionally tend to think of as political action groups. On the surface, one might conclude that all members want to do is get together for a chili cook-off; but scratch beneath the surface, and the body politics are also brewing. Therefore, absolute categories of a "social" versus "political" group are not sufficient to characterize Girth & Mirth, which appears not terribly political to insiders and to insider academics. A Girth & Mirther himself, and a professor of counseling, Michael Loewy is an insider academic. In his co-written chapter on Girth & Mirth, he explains that the group does not have an activist agenda, except as it pertains to identity politics.[21] Other researchers refer to clubs like Girth & Mirth as "appearance organizations" that come together around stigmatized physical characteristics like body shape and size; and people experience "body shame" because of their physical appearance and sexuality.[22]

Girth & Mirth is not necessarily a political action group; the organization tries to salvage big gay men's dignity. Because size is highly
normatively regulated, members push back against obesity as an epi-
demic narrative. Club members are acutely aware of the ways in which
they are not validated by the gay community, and, lacking validation,
they have built a community out of their likeness as stigmatized fellow
sufferers.

Other social movements have also included the body—LGBT, civil
rights, feminism, to name a few. Sizism has a different history, however, because usually when an LGBT group or feminists challenge discrimination they tend to leave their fat sisters and brothers behind
as still excluded from the fight for equal rights. Today, while radical
fat women have carved a niche for themselves in feminist and queer
circles, most LGBT circles have a long way to go in embracing their fat
brethren. Meanwhile, as a multiply marginalized group, gay big men
continue to live in the shadow of the gay community, discriminated
against by everyone, including those one might have assumed would
be their allies.

Considered in the context of the new social movement literature,
which has been pointing toward bringing emotions back into the study
of movements for inclusion, Girth & Mirth represents politics at a personal level.[23] Events organized by the club give members an opportunity
to interact intimately with one another within the comfort zone their
shared culture affords them. Access to intimacy thus becomes a political
act; as feminists well put it in the 1970s, the personal is indeed political.[24]
This is reflected in Girth & Mirth's organizing, though not in the way the
political is typically conceived. Girth & Mirth exemplifies the personal-
political, beyond the historical frame usually considered by traditional
scholars of social movements.

Even though its intention is to draw big gay men out of social isola-
tion, Girth & Mirth does not have a clearly defined political agenda.
However, there are gradations of political engagement among members.
One big man commented that one could consider their work to keep

the club going a political act. In terms of whether the club is built on a politic, he said, "I don't think politics is anywhere near a driving force behind the club. As far as politics goes, it is also not an avoided topic. But it's something that doesn't dominate our club in terms of any of our club rules or philosophies or anything behind the club." Another said, "I think some of the folks in the group are politically aware in a very positive way. One of the subtexts in the group is a kind of interest in advancing the cause of the gay community, like the time several of us marched around the Statehouse."[25]

At the other end of the continuum, some members would rather "steer clear of politics and religion altogether." For instance, the person who is *too* political gets ousted because members would rather simply discuss where to meet for dinner, end of story. In fact, a board member of the local chapter actually had to be quelled, as he had too much of a political agenda. He was ostracized when he tried to use the group as a platform for his views on radical democracy.[26] Radical democracy is different from and arguably extrinsic to the kind of gay and fat politics that exist in Girth & Mirth and similar organizations. Saying that NOLOSE, an organization for fat queers and their allies, for instance, is political because some of its people lobby for Barack Obama, would be to miss the point on the real kind of politics at work in size-positive organizations.

Nonetheless, while gay big men gathering around a meal does not appear to be political on the surface, and even as big men themselves do not necessarily think of their get-togethers around food as political, food intimacy *is* a political act, one that can magnify or mute one's shame. The terms used to describe fat gay men also involve a political spin. As the big man quoted next remarks, one way big men manage their image and the impression they make on others is by playing with words. Indeed, language matters.

Online, "chub" is acceptable—for example, on Chubnet. The chub/chaser stereotype is a big older guy and little younger guy. The classic scenario is the older big fat man and the skinny young chaser. Terminology like "gay," "faggot" (and among African-Americans, "niggah")—just like the black community, we can call each other those terms, but woe to those not in the community who call us that. We call ourselves "chub," "big," "husky," "large," and "fat." Guys in the group may use the first three or "fat," or "big." How people describe things when they play online or strike up a conversation online seems relevant. You're not going to get any response if you say you're fat. "Husky" or "chubby" is OK. If you say "big," then people ask, "How big?" And the conversation degenerates from there [he says with a knowing smile].

Insisting on euphemisms for *fat* may be a cop-out on the part of Girth & Mirthers, as they are rejecting the term used by other groups to politicize. Nevertheless, the speaker still grapples with apologetics, as do I in this book. On the one hand, as a participant observer in the group, I have an emic tendency to use words like *big* or *chub* to refer to the Girth & Mirthers as they themselves would; on the other hand, when I am making more analytical statements as an outsider, I have an etic tendency to use the word *fat*, as I have been significantly influenced by fat studies and fat activism. Indeed, the code-switching I do mirrors the functional ambiguity of the terminology used when talking about body shape and size. It also reflects the situational identity of the Girth & Mirthers.

The speaker's understanding that how he describes body size has ramifications confirms my identification of Girth & Mirthers' practices as being political, despite their own claims that they are apolitical. Other scholars have similarly considered the seeming contradiction in the claim that big men are political even though they disavow politics. Lee Monaghan asserts that some big men's groups provide a politic of pleasure and intimacy, helping people to engage with one another rather than remain isolated. When talking about big handsome men, he advocates thinking about this political conundrum in terms of identity politics.[27]

Fat people fall outside the parameters for ideal sex objects in two major ways: as desexualized beings or as degradable beings.[28] Therefore, big men engaging in sex at all would qualify as transgressive to outsiders, and coming out as both fat and gay truly represents an act of courage.[29] It also involves a change in the party line on fat.[30] In this vein, Girth & Mirth's inclusiveness of a range of body sizes is, in and of itself, a political act. It is also political to put size at the forefront of a shared identity and to make it sexually valuable.

A Normalizing Group

In their desire to be "normal" and to do ordinary things, Girth & Mirthers manage to somewhat repair their stigmatized identity. Before meeting the big men, I had idealized them as outspoken revolutionaries rebelling against gay culture fraught with all its body fascism. Initially, I was baffled by the ordinary activities in which they engaged, like kaffeeklatsches, pot-lucks, or "Big Eats." When I first started attending their events, I was stumped by their run-of-the-mill family-style dining and the game and movie nights. The sheer normality of it all made me apprehensive that my fieldwork would yield uninteresting and useless results, and I would come up empty-handed. After I got to know the big men a little, however, it became clear to me that many simply wanted what conventional folks have and what their gay, "normal-sized" brethren have: an active social life. I understood that was why gay big men engaged in normalized activities.

Then again, while the Girth & Mirthers' events seemed so ordinary, the club appeared to present an uneven kind of normalization. In the strictest sense, normalization usually involves "community membership" with a capital C—it is about mainstreaming folks into the wider community. Over time, I came to appreciate that Girth & Mirth represented a constructed community, or what anthropologists call "fictive kin" or "urban clan" and what members call a "brotherhood" or "chosen family."

The group also had a private clubhouse dimension, holding pool parties at a member's house or pot-lucks in the party room of an apartment complex.

As a sociologist interested in gender and sexuality, I was used to reading about groups with the potential to destabilize the normalization of identity instead of those that mostly reproduce existing conventions. I wondered how this group could seem so contrary to queer theory, which aims to destabilize the normalization of any identity. This led me to question what the big men's return to normalcy meant. In the process of my research, I discovered an unanticipated politic of normalcy, with what seemed to be "exotic" and "deviant" behavior on the flipside. As time went on, I had the good fortune to witness instances of the unmaking of normative expectations. I observed forms of social play, campy-queer behavior, and transgressive carnival performances, which, I realized, were this stigmatized group's attempts at recovering a "normal" life.

There are also the pitfalls that disability studies teach us about normalization, which arguably reconfigures "deviance" as "difference."[31] I learned from the Girth & Mirthers that in trying to pass as "normal," they forgo the right to lament the pain and limitations of living in a sizist gay world. In desiring to blend in, they avoid making a big deal by asking for more comfortable gay spaces; rather, they patronize niche places, like the Bear bar for hirsute gay men, that better accommodate their needs. Yet, even as Girth & Mirthers would like to just go to the "normal" gay bar and not make a scene, if it is too cramped and tight and they cannot get into the bathrooms, they suffer real limitations. In response, many big men just become isolated from the real world and remain more virtually oriented, because size cannot be hidden except over the phone or online.

At times, big men also playfully take a stab at the lack of accommodation for their size. For instance, I learned from a super-chub, an exceptionally big gay man, that one year at the state fair he and a big friend of his challenged the claim of a hardware company that its ladder could safely accommodate the weight of a large person. They wanted to get a free ladder by being allowed to pose standing on the ladder for a picture demonstrating that if it could hold them, it could hold anybody. Though they thought this would make a good advertisement, the salespeople were not amused.

It was not until I had completed my research and produced my first draft that I understood the big men's normalizing activities in terms of what they afforded big gay men. On the surface, their organized events at a special weekend extralocally, such as scantily dressed big men horsing around in a mock beauty contest, may appear a bit outlandish to readers. But really, the big men were simply engaging in gay guys' activities, of which they seemed to want to partake, even if tongue-in-cheek. At the Girth & Mirthers' weekend reunions nationally, a great deal of overt sexualizing tends to take place at the hotel pool.[32] This may seem racier and more amped up than the flirting that may go on at a more conventional pool party. But it is still driven by the most basic of human desires: to be considered a sexually attractive person or, more simply, to be able to unselfconsciously take off one's shirt before entering the pool, a simple act that those of "acceptable" size get to take for granted.

When analyzing my fieldnotes for this book, it also struck me the Girth & Mirthers' taking over a coffee house for one night had foreshadowed what I later discovered in my research, that they were indeed powerful enough organizationally and in their numbers across the nation to take over a hotel for a weekend in order to host a big men's event. These big men's pilgrimages to a weekend reunion may be oversimplified as being driven by their need to go elsewhere to get sex; they go away for the weekend because the club does not offer the opportunity locally. However, the local events and the weekend reunions are not in opposition to each other; they go hand-in-hand. The weekends away are not simply remedies for something missing locally. Going out of town to engage in campy-queer behavior rejuvenates the big men's local activities, just as the quotidian local get-togethers pave the way for the extraordinary weekends.

Finally, at the same time big men appear to have achieved a degree of conventional normalcy through their Girth & Mirth membership, this seems not to assuage yet another—deeper—exclusion, that from the sizist gay community. They therefore frequently meet in normalized spaces like a yuppie coffee house, where oftentimes they receive better treatment, unlike the exclusionary treatment they have come to expect at the local gay coffee house.

In a body-conscious society, we normalize anatomy by changing it—through diets, exercise programs, bariatric and plastic surgery, and various other processes. In contrast, Girth & Mirthers treat the "abnormal" as if it were mostly routine, so that devalued traits like fatness benefit from acquiring a social status they value, such as a long-term friendship or a committed relationship in which they are accepted as they are, without having to make "alterations."[33] In Girth & Mirth circles, members gain much from sharing time with others of common exceptionality—for the most part, they are able to be who they are with less fear of failure or reprisal. One member best summed up the group's efforts at normalization with the following:

Girth & Mirth does things with people who you can be around and be comfortable with, who won't ridicule you, or make you feel uncomfortable in any way. As they say, there's safety in numbers. We do coffee—it's a circle of friends and there's not a clunker in the bunch. You can feel comfortable no matter what. You don't have to feel afraid because you're big. It's a way to have a social group and you don't have to be stuck at home. It's nice for the holidays. You have a place to go. When you're sick, people care. It's a brotherhood, maybe not like the Masons; we don't have a secret handshake. My partner and I have become real close to some couples. It's friends to share with—a chosen family. The thing we choose in our life that provides a place for us.

Herein, I chronicle this special "place" which Girth & Mirth offers big gay men that seems to make such an enormous difference in their lives.

I reflect on the club as both a physical space for socializing and as an abstract, psychological space—or sanctuary—that allows big men to experience normalcy in a size-conscious world. I also explore what the speaker above describes as "comfort," and I discuss the achievement of this in the context of the politics of everyday life.

2

Injuries Big Gay Men Suffer

Boys line up on the field, as the PE teacher yells, "On your marks, get set, ready, go!" They take turns shimmying up bamboo poles, except for a chubby kid who lingers.

The teacher gently urges, "Oyeama, try."

Oyeama shies away from the task: "But I could never climb that pole." Looking back at the pole, he hangs his head in shame.

"Oh now, you shouldn't give up before you try." The teacher walks over to Oyeama's best friend, a skinny, serious-looking boy, and says, "Komatsu, show him how."

"Okay." Komatsu scampers to his friend, as the growing crowd of kids stare. In a gentle voice, he says, "Go on, try." Oyeama grasps the pole and stares at his feet. Komatsu asks, "Why don't you try?"

Oyeama dawdles. "I can't do it," he says.

Komatsu yells, "C'mon!" The pouty child turns to look at him. Komatsu yells again, "C'mon!" He pauses; then, in a soft voice he says, "Do it." Oyeama quickly jumps onto the pole but slides to the ground.

"Once more," Komatsu says. Oyeama leaps back onto the pole. Komatsu uses his back to hoist his friend up. He speaks softly as he tries to catch his breath, "There you go, that's fine, you're doing fine, use your legs." Oyeama looks down. Out of breath, Komatsu grunts: "Try again, grip it tight, don't let go!" Oyeama loses his grip and slides back down the pole, moaning, "Oh, no!"

The complete mortification of walking into gym class as a fat kid and finding out you would be doing something in front of your peers who made you feel uncomfortable: shame. In the case of the characters in the foregoing anecdote, the way out of this shame is through friendship. This scene comes from a black-and-white Japanese film called *Skinny and Fatty*. The film ran regularly on Saturday afternoons in the 1960s and '70s as part of the CBS Children's Film Festival.[1] As the story goes, Komatsu, a skinny poor boy, excels at school and sports and draws out his fat, introverted friend Oyeama. The two become an unlikely team in athletic competitions. I learned of this movie from a middle-aged man I met in Girth & Mirth, who struggles with his confidence over his weight, as do most others in the group. He mentioned having seen the film as an adolescent, and that it made a lasting impression on him.

Another Girth & Mirther shared his childhood experience of being bullied. His memories of the bullying were cloudy, as he may have blocked the physical abuse, though he vividly remembered the name-calling. As he said, "Every year it seemed like the kids found a new name to call me. There were days I would go home from school in tears. Sometimes it came to physical blows or there was a physical altercation, a kid hitting me or something like that." As Monaghan points out, when boys bully fat kids in school, their behavior parodies and reproduces "definitional practices and body pedagogies evidenced in the surrounding sizist society where the obese are positioned as slothful, gluttonous, uncivilized and deservedly discredited on account of their assumed 'poor lifestyle choices.'"[2] In essence, kids quickly learn to reproduce what they see going on around them in the larger society, which demonizes fat people.

This is not to suggest that all of the big men who are members of Girth & Mirth were fat as children. However, like this speaker, gay big men not only experience social injuries and bullying, such as feeling shamed and excluded, but also have to deal with the injuries of marginalization and desexualization they suffer within the gay community. While all of the wrongs they endure are hurtful, they are especially so when coming from one's own social identity group.

Fatty's mortification story in the film would strongly resonate with members of Girth & Mirth, whose experiences of "everyday shame" have come to affect their sentient or feeling bodies. Elspeth Probyn defines this type of shame as the body's painful awareness of being out of place in everyday life that occurs when bodies are unable to conform, leaving them nowhere to hide.[3] In sociological terms, fat's obtrusiveness makes it nearly impossible to pass as "thin" even with traditional strategies like girdling or covering.[4] Thus, "fat" provokes strong body policing, particularly among gay men.[5] "Normals" rarely overlook real-life "Fatties" in public, though this is of course historically and contextually dependent.

Kathleen LeBesco points out that there are strands of fat scholarship so hell-bent on showing fat in a positive light that they are willing to overlook the story of woundedness.[6] When this is done, however, "fat-positive" scholars have a difficult time accounting for those fat people who resort to fad diets or bariatric surgery and label them "traitors." They do not want to acknowledge the overriding pull of the "fat negative": It is depressing to be marginalized for one's size. I myself fell into this trap, not wanting to write about woundedness, especially because the moniker "Girth & Mirth" stands for being fat and happy. It is essential, however, to understand big men's social injuries and why they have to work so hard to reconfigure themselves and why they still would fall short of fat-positive standards. Likewise, Monaghan discusses accounts of stigma that heterosexual men incur in relation to their dieting careers, referring to their wounds as "wartime injuries," given the current "War on Obesity" in the industrialized world.[7] In this chapter, I discuss the injuries—shame, marginalization, exclusion, and desexualization—inflicted upon big men. I first examine how they suffer in mainstream society as a result of their ample size; I then focus more deeply on big gay men's experiences of exclusion and the consequent injuries they suffer within gay society.

Injuries Big Gay Men Experience in Mainstream Society
Everyday Encounters with Discrimination

Everyday incivilities that gay big men frequently encounter within the main include unfriendly and disrespectful treatment in the marketplace and discrimination and denial of health care in hospitals and doctors' offices. Many have come to expect this kind of mistreatment and the daily hassles that come with being fat. As one Girth & Mirther put it, in some cases, "Even if big men are not treated differently, the perception might be there because they almost expect it. When I was young, every time I had gym, I almost began to expect the mistreatment. It's just something that comes by rote."

In American society, size often intersects with a class-based assumption that being "overweight" equals being poor. One Girth & Mirther referred to the exclusion big men experience in department stores as "profiling." He described getting the cold shoulder from salespeople when he went to buy a suit at the mall, much as the Julia Roberts character, a prostitute, did when she went clothes shopping on Rodeo Drive in *Pretty Woman*.[8]

> I really wanted to buy this suit at Elder-Beerman [a Midwest-based U.S. department store chain], but I couldn't get served. I was somehow invisible to the salespeople. I finally gave up and went to J. C. Penney, got good service, and bought a suit. The next day, I returned to Elder-Beerman. On my first visit, I had pretty much dressed casual. This time, I was dressed in business attire. People rushed to help me. I said, "When I was here yesterday, no one would assist me. I had seen a suit I really wanted to buy and was planning on dropping around 400 bucks." Then I walked out.

This account illustrates how this big man felt discriminated against because of a combination of his size and attire. He went on to say, "No one offered me service the first day because the salespeople had profiled me as the sloppy fat guy who didn't have any money and didn't deserve to be acknowledged as a customer." Treating people "as if they were not there at all, as objects not worthy of a glance," is what Goffman calls "'nonperson' treatment."[9] The speaker above further explained that the salesperson had made an assumption, based on his appearance, that if he was fat, he must also be poor and therefore could not afford the suit. The narrative became complicated when this big man returned the next day wearing his new attire, much as the Julia Roberts character had, and confronted the salesperson much to his satisfaction. This minor victory is not the way the story usually goes, however.

Fat profiling, broadly classified, occurs when generalizations are made about an entire category of people as having a vast array of moral failings, based solely on physical characteristics such as size and appearance. Sociologically speaking, fat assumes a master status, where its stigmatizing character becomes a controlling category. Following Goffman, Erich Goode argues that "normals" tend to fixate on a particular negative trait. However, fat takes on a broadly perceived focus. As a stigmatizing trait, it is rarely the only characteristic people find fault with in someone; it also comes with the assumption that the person possesses a multitude of other associated "defects." The one trait—fat—supersedes all others and gets lumped together with a whole host of imperfections. We could also think of the merely descriptive term *fat* as being reified to the extent that if one is ascribed this status, then one is thought to possess all of its negative characteristics, which are socially appointed.[10] Thus, "normal" people make a wide range of negative assumptions regarding fat people: that "Fatty" cannot perform in sports (or occupations); as in the "Pretty Fatman" example, that fat people are slobs; or that they are unsexy and deserve to be taken advantage of.

Big men are not only profiled and ignored by salespeople, but they also are injured when they suffer public indictment for "taking up too much space." One Girth & Mirther described being publicly stigmatized and harassed for his size by a total stranger. He said, "I was getting on the bus one time and the person beside me just kept complaining, 'You're too big, you're half on my seat, too.' I was in my seat, I may have filled it, but, you know, I wasn't halfway on his seat." This big man clearly suffered the indignity of public harassment that was inadvertently provoked by his appearance. He had to endure a stranger's unsolicited remarks just because of his ample size.

At other times, one's size can garner public indictment that comes with the façade of being justified. For example, regardless of gender and sexual orientation, fat people are excluded from amusement park rides. Often, there are "politically correct" signs like those one sees in family fun parks that read along the lines of, "This ride may not be able to accommodate guests of exceptional size." Furthermore, theme parks are careful not to specify precisely what "exceptional size" is. Granted, they may be making a reasonable request in warning their guests "for their own safety," and, after all, a business must protect itself against a potential lawsuit if a ride were to malfunction. But adding insult to injury, only after they anxiously wait in line, sometimes for an hour, not knowing whether they can squeeze into a particular amusement park ride, do fat people find out they do not fit. So when their turn finally comes and they discover they cannot lock down the safety bars on the ride, they are forced to get back out, humiliated. One big man described his experience at an amusement park as follows:

> Now, where I'm from, we have Pride Night at Kings Island Amusement Park. Talk about the stigmas of being big, my God, some of us can't ride the rides. Face it—we're too big. The safety features don't allow us to fit in the thing properly. I don't blame them, it's a hazard, but it's humiliating. A lot of times, we'll go with a group of people and it gets to be a big joke, "How many rides did *you* get kicked off of?"

Having developed some immunity to "the stigmas of being big," this Girth & Mirther appears able to stave off such a mortifying experience with good humor by calling it "a big joke." However, this big man must still live with the felt repercussions of sizism. As a man of "exceptional size," he has been transformed into a safety problem anticipated by the ride's seemingly polite and innocuous sign. Indeed, one would have a hard time arguing with signs proclaiming "for your own safety"; even the big man thus transformed by the sign cannot find fault with it. Toril Moi describes this transformation as symbolic annihilation, which is "literally unrecognizable as violence" because it seems legitimate and is taken for granted, obscuring what could be challenged as discrimination.[11] Thus, the warning gets accepted as a "social fact."[12] Sociologically speaking, this is what Bourdieu calls "symbolic violence, a gentle violence, imperceptible and invisible even to its victims."[13] This is why the big man who has to be kicked off the rollercoaster does not question the unaccommodating size of the seat.

Health-Care Discrimination

Health-care providers are also guilty of sizism. For instance, medical professionals may deny care altogether, or they may provide it differentially to fat patients. They may fixate on size and ignore the presenting symptoms. Furthermore, they may make broad generalizations about whether a person is healthy or unhealthy. One Girth & Mirther spoke of three different big men who were rejected for surgery (gastric bypass, bad knee, and back problems). He said:

> They went to the doctor, who told them, "Well, you're too big for us to operate on. Your heart will be crushed by your own weight as you lie on the table. So we can't treat you until you lose weight." And that's pretty much paraphrased by each of the three different guys. So what they're left with is a health problem and a weight problem and no one who will help them along with the rotten judgmental treatment they just walked out the door with, because they feel that much worse from what was said to them. And if they felt hopeless when they walked in, they would feel even worse when they walked out.

Another Girth & Mirther shared the following encounter he had with the medical community, in which his size became an obstacle to his receiving medical treatment.

> I've had knee problems in the past. This one surgeon I went to, who was like the top orthopedic guy in the city, said he wouldn't replace my knee at that time because, he says, "My table only goes up to 320 pounds for physical therapy and you, my friend, are over that." And that sort of pissed me off. My retort to him was, "Okay, I understand where you're coming from and I appreciate your position, but if I were brought into an emergency room from a horrible car accident and my knees were crushed because the engine went back into the passenger compartment, would you replace my knees?"

As the big man expected, the orthopedic surgeon's answer was "Yes," which was evidence that he was discriminating against this big man. He had humiliated him by telling him he was too big for the table. Incidentally, at six foot one and 305–310 pounds, this big man was actually under the weight limit, and he knew the surgeon was brazenly denying him health care as a condition of his size and of the circumstance—his visit to the doctor not being for a dire emergency. Too often, big men's needs are denied because of the perception that fat people are a burden and an inconvenience to the health-care system. Thus they have no recourse but to reason with their doctors for their health care.

The same big man related an encounter he had in the emergency room, where his weight and size overtly took precedence over his presenting symptoms. His being visibly overweight caused doctors to fixate on his size and ignore the intense pain in his abdomen. Focusing on and blaming his weight, the ER personnel assumed he must be having a heart attack. They consequently *re*-categorized his abdominal pain as "heartburn," which is one of the symptoms of heart attack, though atypical. He recounted:

> I knew I was passing a kidney stone. We go to the hospital, I'm in pain, I'm in agony, I'm sitting there, I can't stand up, I can't walk; they put me

in the wheelchair and they keep asking me if I am feeling a heaviness in my chest. I said, "No-o-o, it's in my gut. It's an abdominal pain." And you know, they keep asking me things indicating they think it's a heart attack. They say, "Well, sometimes a heart attack can disguise itself as abdominal pain." I'm like, "Oh, okay, I've never heard of that." And so, the first thing they do is they run an EKG on me. Then finally, they decide I am *not* having a heart attack; they admit it must be something else. So then, they put me back in the emergency room and take me back to do all these *other* tests, and find out, yes, it's indeed a kidney stone.

In this encounter, the patient knew where his pain was located and what he had, but he could not get the ER staff to hear him. His frustration on top of the excruciating pain of passing a kidney stone was the ER doctor's assuming it was a heart attack, thereby ordering a battery of unnecessary tests and needlessly prolonging his pain, though perhaps under the guise of defensive medicine. This example of sizism in health-care provision parallels the literature on gender inequality in health care.[14]

The particular doctor-patient interactions just recounted represent a larger social problem: the difficulty of people who are "overweight" getting doctors and medical professionals to pay attention to anything other than their fat. It is the classification of patients into "fat" versus "normal" that creates everyday shame. Under such circumstances, which make fatness the primary object of scrutiny and diagnosis, the patient cannot be an ordinary patient but is always, and already, profiled as a "fat" patient first. This sizism also has strong parallels with some of the feminist literature on female patients' encounters with sexist male doctors.[15]

Injuries Big Men Experience within Gay Society
Gay–on–Big Gay Discrimination

Social injuries incurred by being fat are not exclusive to gay big men. These injuries, however, are compounded in the case of gay big men, for whom size and sexuality, though different issues, intersect, adding another ripple to their injuries. One Girth & Mirther shared that in heteronormative society, big men are at least recognized as "gay," whereas in gay circles, they are seen only as "fat." As he said, "In society as a whole, I don't think people focus on the fact that if they see a group of big gay men it's not that it's *big* gay men, it's that it's *gay* men. What society still sees is just a bunch of gay men. But within the gay community, they see us as, 'Oh, it's a bunch of *big* guys.'"

Thus, in addition to the obstacles they encounter in mainstream society just for being fat, big men suffer from being relegated to the margins of gay society as well. Gay men sometimes inflict suffering upon one another by upholding a sizist criterion in choosing a sex partner. Several big men confided in me in many different ways how it hurts *worse* to be excluded within the gay community, because the exclusion is perpetrated by their own. They shared how they feel *more* hurt when they are overlooked in the gay community than when they are simply ignored in mainstream society. As one of them said, "In the gay community it's the most troubling because you're treated differently and you're overlooked. People can be pretty cruel, sometimes. You'd think we'd be the ones to know better because as a group, as gay people we've been criticized or harassed plenty. We should know better than to treat our own that way."

I witnessed firsthand the reality of this gay–on–big gay discrimination at one of the group's charity bar nights. When the Girth & Mirth president and I walked out to the patio, we encountered a group of average-sized men congregated around the heater. However, as soon as the two of us sidled up to the heater, they all split. With one fell swoop, the big man had cleared the patio. He recognized what had just taken place and ruefully mumbled something to me. I tried to explain away the others' departure by suggesting that in the context of the Bear bar it might have been because my slender build had led them to dismiss me as a little stuck-up "twink," therefore not a "real" man. But the awkwardness of the situation could not be denied. Feeling really bad for him, I hugged him. For that split second, I was no longer "the researcher." Then a guy ran out onto the patio and proceeded to get sick and throw up, which quickly snapped us out of our misery. Considering that the Girth & Mirthers themselves were hosting this particular event, one might have trusted it to be a safe haven. Alternatively, it is not clear why the men left the heater, as there is no real evidence they were fatphobic. However, a tenet of sociological training is the Thomas Theorem: "If [people] define situations as real, they are real in their consequences."[16]

In *Such a Pretty Face: Being Fat in America*, Millman discusses at length women's worries about and struggles with their weight. The fitting words in Millman's title in fact came up in one of my interviews with a Girth & Mirther. Making the connection between heterosexual women's experience of disembodiment and that of fat gay men, this Girth & Mirther said to me, "Oh, that's the most horrible thing to say, 'lovely girl, such a pretty face,' you know, 'big as a barn.'" Gay men, like heterosexual women, grapple with their relationship to food, as both feel self-conscious about their looks and physiques usually more than heterosexual men do.[17] While in her 250-page work Millman does not address issues fat men might have with weight (except for a 10-page appendix), she does remark, "[I]f any group of people worry about their weight more than American women, it is probably gay men. . . . [O]verweight gay men share with all overweight women the burden of imputed psychological interpretations."[18]

Historically, gay men have not enjoyed the same leeway as heterosexual men with regard to fatness. They are marginalized for not conforming to rigid bodily standards used to stratify their community by size. Like other body aesthetics, the gay male aesthetic privileges lean, taut, muscular upper bodies, and this standard is rewarded within gay culture such as in clubs and commercial representations.[19] Gay visual culture is hard to live up to, with its focus on worshipping "perfect" bodies of male models in not only pornography magazines but also in health and physique magazines that gay men consume as homoerotic. As in mainstream society, gay obsession with fat is exacerbated by advertisements that idolize the fit and muscular frame, contributing to gay men's dissatisfaction with their bodies. One Girth & Mirther shared his self-consciousness about not fitting the "gay mold."

> I feel like an outcast in gay society. I don't feel comfortable at all. To me, it's for young, thin, gorgeous people, and I don't fit in there; it makes me feel uncomfortable. I'm older, I'm heavier, and I don't fit the gay mold, as you would say. You know, every time you look at a gay magazine, you see a hunky, muscle-bound, young, gorgeous man; I don't fit that mold. So, I'm gay, I'm big, and I can't help who I am.

Because many gay men prioritize personal appearance, they spend an inordinate amount of time and resources trying to modify their looks through working out, cosmetic surgery, tanning, and hair restoration or removal.[20] Commercial images exclude "imperfect" gay bodies—namely, fat, old, or disabled—and divide men along these lines. And out of this litany of obsessions gay men have with their appearance, fat tends to remain a constant.

Fat gay men find it difficult to identify with the monolithic image of the gay body. There is little to no representation in the media or in any gay clubs of big gay men as being sexy. This leaves gay big men with very few role models. It is harder for a big man to make his sexual debut when he cannot easily recognize anyone in the gay scene who looks like himself. For instance, one Girth & Mirther told me about his discomfort in the leather club where he felt like a sexual outsider or a misfit, because there was no one else around with his body type. As he said, "I had previously done the 'leather thing.' The leather clubs were okay, but not many big guys were there. A chub tied down to a bondage table would be hot with the flesh bulging between the ropes but I never got to see it; it was always me on the table. That was fun and everything, but as a big person, I was not exactly comfortable there." This big man went on to share with me that, in fact, his discomfort as a sexual outsider within the gay scene led him to form the local chapter of Girth & Mirth, together with a friend of his, another big man.

One Girth & Mirther's story about Gay Days at Disney World provides another example of discomfort with existing images of gay men that do not easily invite a fat gay man to identify with them. He imagined even if he could finally be in an environment where he could freely hold hands with his boyfriend, his weight would be a deterrent. So in our interview, he elaborated on his disappointment with Gay Days. The story he shared illustrates how his fatness was not a detriment to him as a straight man; however, now as a gay man, he felt it does restrict him.[21]

> The bar we go to has videos of Gay Day celebrations, and it's like a giant dance party at one of the water parks or in the park after they've closed. And I watched the video, thinking this is gonna be great. But I was never so uncomfortable in my life as when watching it. Everybody there was toned or muscular in Speedos, there was hardly anybody in a boxer-style swim trunk; there were no bellies to be seen. The music was great, the lights were great, everything was great, but it's like as a fat guy, would I feel comfortable going to that? No, because there were no other fat guys there. And if you're the only fat guy who goes to something like that, people are gonna stare.
>
> We might still go to Gay Days someday, but it's gonna be a while. I wouldn't, I would love to be able to go to Disney World 'cause I love to go to Disney, I used to go two to three times a year with my wife, honest to God. You should see all the Disney crap sitting here in the apartment. I would love to be able to go to Disney World and walk hand-in-hand with my partner down Main Street, and go on the rides with him, but now that I've seen what the Gay Day thing is like, I don't think I could go.

The layers of injury are apparent in the story this big man relayed. First, for being gay, he cannot freely have a romantic time at Disney World except one weekend per year. And second, for being fat, he and his partner cannot fathom attending even that one special weekend because they would become a spectacle. He continued to elaborate on the complexities of being doubly marginalized:

I mean, we feel comfortable in certain areas of town walking around holding hands. During Gay Pride, we held hands at Bat-n-Rouge, the drag queen softball game. We have no problem with that in certain areas of town. We wouldn't do it everywhere, but we're very comfortable with that. But in Disney World, where I would want to be able to do that, I would not. Normally, I would not do that there, because of the stigma of being gay; and during Gay Days at Disney, we *could* hold hands, but I wouldn't even go, because of being big.

Some big men feel forced to make the decision to settle for an asexual existence. Feeling desexualized for being fat and not fitting the gay mold, they choose to pass their time at their jobs and spend more time with their parents and children. One Girth & Mirther said:

I was at that point in my life where I was just over the whole gay scene. I would go online and talk to people, and they were like, "Oh, you're too big, I don't want to talk to you." Then you'd start feeling like you're not part of that scene anymore. So I just disconnected myself from everything, and I started spending more time with my family. And I ended up getting a second job and I worked seven days a week because, what else was there for me to do? I didn't feel comfortable going to a bar because I was big. I didn't feel like I was there for a purpose. Nobody was going to hit on me, so why should I be there? So, I threw myself into my work, my family, and my friends and I let that be it. That was going to be my life.

Another injury fat gay men are more likely to share with fat women is their experience of desexualization, in which they are deprived of sex appeal and are discouraged from expressing their sexuality. What is worse is that unsexy associations are linked to fatness. As Millman hints in her book, big men feel they are out of the running in the sexual marketplace.[22] One Girth & Mirther spoke about being young and living in a college town. He said, "People are at that age when they're discovering themselves. If you're gay and skinny, your prospects are better in the gay world. You'll be popular—fresh meat, as it were. But if you're fat, chubby, husky, you're not as popular; you won't get the looks or be cruised as often. People don't acknowledge large people. It's harder to be big and gay." Another big man lamented desexualization's leading to dehumanization. As he told me,

> When you're gay and big, the discrimination is horrible. People won't talk to you because you're big. I mean you don't want to go to bed with me, you might not be attracted to me, but my God, I'm a human being and you can't treat me like one? Just because you don't want to go to bed with somebody doesn't mean you can't talk to them?

And if a big man *does* get acknowledged and enters into a relationship with a gay man of a socially acceptable weight, sometimes his partner will be reluctant to be seen with him in public because he will be ashamed of the partner's size. The relationship will be kept on the down-low, because there is shame associated with owning up to it in public. Goffman's "courtesy stigma" seems particularly relevant here.[23] It illuminates how, rather than being perceived as deviant for associating with a fat person, closeted admirers choose to manage their stigma for this potentially discrediting attachment to their reputation by concealing it. One big man shared the following on the subject of becoming someone's dirty little secret because one's lover is ashamed of being seen dating a fat guy:

> It's sort of like a straight guy who wants to have sex with a gay guy—at least, allegedly straight. And, they don't want anyone to know they're having sex; they're embarrassed, it's like, "I'll date you in private, we'll go to your house, or to my house, but I don't want to be seen with you in public." It's like that with dating big guys, too. Some guys will date you in private because they don't want people to know they like bigger guys. And I had a guy who approached me who was very enjoyable, but once I made the comment "Hey, let's go out to dinner at this gay restaurant," he backed

off. It seemed to always be, "Well, if we're gonna go out somewhere to eat, let's go way up north, way out of the way to where nobody will know me."

Another big man lamented having been emotionally abused by former partners. He explained how one of his ex-boyfriends used to behave like a bad boy and openly date other people. Apparently, he enjoyed flaunting it. This Girth & Mirther shared the following about another ex of his:

> One of my exes was Portuguese. The guy was hot and he was thin and he was gorgeous and he was with *me*! But he also dated four other guys while we were living together. And I think it had to do with me being fat; he figured I wouldn't find anybody else. Or I wouldn't date anybody else, because I couldn't find anybody as good as him, or as good-looking as him, or whatever.

Much to this big man's chagrin, it was not only his boyfriend's machismo working against their relationship, but also he himself was relegated to the role of a "daddy" to this misbehaving handsome bad boy.[24]

Similarly, one Girth & Mirther remarked on the assumption that if one is a fat gay man, he is a beggar, who therefore cannot be a chooser. As he said, "Little gay guys think, 'You're a big guy, so therefore you probably don't have a lot of guys who pay attention to you. So you should be okay with any kind of attention you get. Be happy you're getting any attention at all.'" One big man similarly described the dehumanizing experience of this beggar-chooser dynamic.

> When I was much bigger, I had one guy who was after me because his comment was, "You got a fat ass, and you can't get any, so you'll enjoy my cock." Little did he realize I didn't need his dick. Those are the wrong intentions as far as I'm concerned. It's the same principle as, "Oh, that guy, he's mentally retarded, he's easy prey." It's the same thing, and to me that's deplorable behavior. Unfortunately, there are guys who will look at it like, "Oh, they're a big guy, they don't get much sex, this is a guaranteed port

of entry. I'll just use their mouth or ass as a cum repository." It's like, okay, but there's also a front side to me, there's a brain to me, too.

Luckily, in the case of this big man, he was strong and self-assured enough to recognize and avoid being dehumanized as a mere receptacle. When gay men impose the submissive role on big men simply because they are fat, the talk gets loaded as in heterosexual discourse, corresponding with active-submissive gender role expectations. Heterosexism operates on the myth that all gay men are effeminate, and vice versa. The irony is, there is also the assumption that partners in same-sex relationships still take on traditional gender roles, and in the case of big men, fat amounts to degradable femininity.

Likewise, Millman mentions fat women's vulnerability to sexual exploitation. She writes, when "a fat woman falls outside the parameters of ideal sex object, . . . [she] is often viewed as . . . an easy lay, a suitable target for lewdness and degradation."[25] College men who prey on fat women and brag about it to their buddies call this "hogging," which can escalate into a degraded sexuality, another form of gender violence.[26] Hogging tends to happen in the gay world, as well. In other words, fat gets gendered when gay men, like heterosexual women, fall under the male gaze and are sexually evaluated by men. Interestingly, as Millman observes, even straight men, if they are fat, are emasculated by other men, and oddly not in the eyes of women.[27] That is, both for heterosexual women and for straight men, *and* as I am arguing here, for gay men, being fat as it affects one's sex appeal is most frequently judged by *men*—long recognized by feminists to be an oppressive arrangement. As Michael Kimmel articulates it so well in his book *Guyland*, men perform their masculinity for other men, who are the ultimate judges of it.[28]

Given these dynamics, gay men stigmatize those who do not adhere to rigid bodily standards. These boundaries perpetuate gender inequality.[29] For instance, in personals gay men often advertise for body qualities in potential partners, which they link to gender, such as "Should be in shape, please *no* fats or femmes!" Based on such requests, failing to be "height-weight proportionate" deviates from how a gay body "ought to *look*."[30] Fat feminizes male features, threatening masculinity and departing from the archetype of the disciplined hard body.[31] It makes men's genitals appear smaller and causes men to develop breasts and hips, their physicality ultimately betraying them as it reinforces the effeminate label.[32] In order to gain acceptance and to ward off the stigma of being fat or femme, gay men often invoke rigid gender roles, making the "straight-acting, masculine" male highly desirable.[33] In this way, they create in and out groups based on both bodily requirements and gender expectations.

Also, as Millman found in her study of fat women, fat renders not only the whore but also the Madonna, as it becomes negatively associated with effeminacy.[34] This is exemplified in one big man's holiday tryst with a small man described below. As he told me, he prefers men smaller than he, though he sometimes feels as if he were typecast in a motherly role.

> For instance, cuddling—I'm the one who's holding on to the other person. I'm not really sure how to describe that dynamic. But it seems if it's not a gender thing, then what is it? It's almost like a motherly role. Like last year on my cruise, I met this guy and this dude was tiny. I mean, five foot nothing, just tiny. And we were sitting outside on the ship and it's like, two in the morning. I'm sitting down and he's literally sitting against me in my lap. It was kind of cute, actually. But like, I'm this big guy and he's this little dinky guy, and he's literally in my lap. I'm sitting down, and he's cuddled up like a koala bear would grab onto a tree.

This kind of narrative was in fact rare, because the local group of Girth & Mirth I studied tended to consist of big men who preferred big men, and this kind of oppositional pairing was outside their immediate experience. Big gay men can certainly associate bulky males with masculinity; however, among the larger gay community, they tend to negatively associate fat with effeminacy. For example, one interpretation of "drag" is that it is a mockery of women. This interpretation relies on the notion that the classic drag queens display "fat tits" and "big hips."

Big-on-Big Discrimination

Then again, even big gay men are of two minds with regard to fat. For example, as one Girth & Mirther told me, "There are chubs, and then there's the 'super-chub'—the guy Richard Simmons wants to get his hands on and save." In chub/chaser culture, this is simply a "really big" chub. When I asked him, "Do you see big men being more closely associated with femininity or masculinity?" he acknowledged he sometimes does a double-take when a super-chub whom he would normally peg as "effeminate" presents as masculine. He articulated how he waffles between judging men much bigger than he as effeminate and judging them as masculine. He said:

> Some of the big super-chubs are usually very effeminate, but not always. If you go to the big men's Super Weekend, you'll see some guys who are just big and very effeminate, flaming queens from the get-go. Then there's Bobby from Texas.[35] God, I hope he shows up this year. He's big and he's just, he's all man. That's the only way to put it. He's all man, but sexually, a bottom. Though to look at him, you wouldn't think so.
>
> Along these lines, though, I don't find super-chubs attractive. Bottom line: personality-wise, you can have the best personality in the world, but if you're very, very, very large, a lot bigger than I am, I probably would not be attracted to you. I'll still be your friend, you're a human being, I believe in that kind of thing, but . . . .

As this big man articulated it, fat at its extreme skews gender perceptions, and one's taste for body types bigger than one's own has its limits. Apparently, this big man, who is himself just over 300 pounds, drew the line at "super-chubs." So, there appears to be a hierarchy even among big gay men that leads to within-group injuries, as well.

Some big men struggle with a sense of guilt for not being attracted to other big men. One Girth & Mirther whom I interviewed elaborated on his preference for smaller men and his conflicted feelings about it. He seemed guilt-ridden about being exclusionary, especially because other big men in chatrooms accused him of being sizist. He said:

> I'm frustrated that I am overlooked or excluded from certain things, but if I actually look at myself, I'm sort of doing the same thing: I'm a big guy who's looking for little guys, so I'm excluding big guys because they're big. You actually could say I tend to be even more exclusive in my choice of partners than most. When I see someone big, in my mind I almost automatically say, "They're not an option." In chatrooms, I actually got a scolding 'cuz they kind of look at it as though I'm being prejudiced against other big guys. But that's not the case, and I don't have a problem with other big guys in terms of friendship and things like that. It's just that I'm not attracted to them.
>
> I personally grapple with whether I have some sort of prejudice against big guys. So, what gives me the right to be upset that I'm being excluded if I myself exclude other people? It's a hard thing to figure out, and I have been doing a lot of soul-searching about how I am being unfair to big guys by excluding them in terms of dating. So how can I be upset that I'm excluded from the dating pool because of my size?

This big man wrestled with whether his sexual preference for "normal"-sized bodies stems from his own internalized fatphobia. Some big men confessed that they want to dissociate themselves from other people who are fat, as if fatness were contagious. The dread of becoming fat renders some people reluctant to associate with fat people, lest they contract "fatness," a fear most likely fueled by their own self-hatred. Yet one cannot expect big men to be any different from anyone else in terms of having a physical attraction for a particular body shape and size, because to a great degree, desire for or aversion to a particular body type is socially constructed.

Given gay men's fatphobia, it was not surprising that there were fewer thin admirers in the local group of Girth & Mirth I studied. Little reliable information exists on the ratio of big men to admirers who attend these groups. Because the role of admirer tends to be associated with a slimmer physique, gay men's media and limited literature exaggerate the oppositional pairing of chubs and chasers (admirers with thinner builds who find big, chubby men attractive). However, my observations of online and actual communities do not support this. I discovered, as it happens, that in most partner selection a reasonable number of big men opt for relationships with physically similar partners; hence, the online personals expression "chub4chub." I also found that several men attend events as romantic couples.

Some big gay men also choose to deny their weight and remain in the fat closet, although it is clearly difficult to hide their undeniably visible bodies. Nonetheless, as I learned from the big man in the following quote, this big-on-big rejection can be hurtful. As he related to me, he was incredulous that a man who weighs 425 pounds would reject *him*, who weighed at least 100 pounds less.

> I had somebody online say I was a fat slob. But he weighed 425 pounds and that's a lot more than I do. And *he* wasn't interested in *me*? And I was just mortified that somebody who was larger than me had made that comment. And I blogged about it, but I guess that's not uncommon. People said probably after he did that, he put me on "ignore" so I couldn't contact him any further.

It appears this big man was not so much hurt by being rejected by a gay man but, rather, disconcerted more because his ego was bruised when the rejection came from someone bigger than him. People generally expect that they will be able to date those who are physically similar to them. They tend to assume they will be attractive to those who look like them. By the same token, the speaker had assumed he ought to be able to be desirable to *at least* those fatter than him. Therefore, he was astonished to be rejected by someone who weighed about one hundred pounds more than he did. He went on to tell me, "I assumed this guy probably talked to one of his skinny friends about how this big guy was chasing him or whatever. Who knows? It really hurt me. It really hurt me."

Similar to the interpersonal rejection described above, there also appears to be a larger big-on-big public rejection. Girth & Mirthers reported to me that when they try to recruit other gay big men to join the club, they sometimes are equally shocked that some do not want to join. It may be that these men disidentify with a group that celebrates being fat and happy, and they may not wish to be associated and seen with a group of fellow sufferers. Therefore, big gay pride is a difficult subject position to sell, and those attempting to do so expose themselves to public rejection on behalf of the group, as if it were not already hard enough on them to be personally rejected.

> A lot of people don't identify with Girth & Mirth. I talked to a guy online one time, and he was my height and weighed 350 pounds, and I'm like, "Oh, you *know* this is Girth & Mirth," and I explained about the club. And he was like, "I'm not a big guy." And I'm thinking, "Okay, if you say so." I wanted to type back, "*Yeah* you are—you're in *denial.*" But then I thought, "Well, maybe he doesn't see himself that way, and whatever his issues are and whatever his reasons are, they're his." They see us at these events, and see us being who we are, but some still won't cross the line and accept, "Yeah, I'm a big gay man." But that's their loss.

Indeed, as the speaker guessed, self-denial can be a real impediment to big men's trying to organize. In their efforts to promote their club by handing out their cards to big gay men on the sidelines, Girth & Mirthers are surprised and hurt when some big men seem to be insulted by being pegged as "one of us." One member said:

> One year, we tried to hand out our cards along the parade route to big guys we saw standing there. We'd say, "Hey, come march with us, you're a big guy, you're good-looking, get out here," and, you know, people were offended. Some people were just shocked we had identified them as one of us, and they didn't want to be.

From these accounts, I gathered that theirs appears to be a club they cannot get anyone to join so easily, given the heightened stigma of being fat within the larger gay community and the internalization of fatphobia. For example, a big gay man who shaved my head at the salon remarked to me that he went out to a gay bar and they were having a lube-wrestling contest. He said there were a lot of big men there and he remarked that he did not identify with the big men's groups "because they act all proud about their bodies and I know my body and I know my limits and what looks good and what does not." He clearly did not assume the subject position of "fat and proud"; rather, he had internalized fat as unflatter-ing, and therefore a limitation. One Girth & Mirther expressed a theory as to why young gay men do not join the club. In his opinion, it may have something to do with fat's symbolizing getting old. He said, "A lot of younger gay men view our club as gross, disgusting, too big, or too old. They separate themselves from us by saying, 'I don't want anything to do with them.'"

Not only is recruitment a challenge, but big men also run into verbal assaults on their group, becoming targets of derision. At a Girth & Mirth Pride parade-planning meeting, after discussing plans for the group's participation in the annual Gay Pride parade, one member shared his experience of shaming that took him by surprise: "I was in a chatroom the other night and some users started attacking Girth & Mirth, saying we were an embarrassment to the gay community. They said the only reason people clap for us at the Pride parade is because we're such a spectacle." Indeed, as Millman observes, "[W]hen a homosexual man is fat, he is often viewed in the gay community as not having sufficient 'self-pride.'"[36]

If Girth & Mirthers are denied claim to Pride, then as Probyn explains, the shame of being fat "makes apparent the ways in which radically differ-ent positioned selves are [deemed] contagious."[37] At times, for example, while I mingled among the Girth & Mirthers as a participant observer, my thinness stood out at such a polar opposite to the bigness of the men

I was studying that one guy remarked on how I needed to "eat a pork chop or two," and others wondered whether I had gained weight yet from hanging out with them.

More often than not, however, the belief that fatness is contagious can get ugly. The following story from a Girth & Mirther in the Pride parade illustrates how extreme and wacky the fear of contamination can get. At an annual Pride celebration, a religious protester heckled the Girth & Mirthers in the parade, not recognizing the irony of what he was saying, considering he himself was big and, presumably, straight. With a loudspeaker, he barked from the sidelines: "Oh, my God, here come the fat guys! No wonder you're gay, there's no woman who would have you. No wonder there are so many lesbians in the community! You guys don't know how to take care of your bodies." Triply contagious! Apparently, gay big men can not only make people fat, they can also make others gay or lesbian. Sadly, unlike what Lory Britt and David Heise suggest, this shame does not diffuse positively. It does *not* create empathy, nor does it recruit new members through emotional contagion, nor is it about crowd contagion; rather, it inspires onlookers to further humiliate the big men and perpetuate their shame.[38]

Big men are also left out of media coverage of Pride. For instance, when it came to covering the annual parade in the gay "rag," out of a total of thirty-four snapshots there were no pictures of the Girth & Mirth bunch participating in the festivities. In the words of one member, "In the local gay publications, they had pictures from Pride, but there were no men from our group in any of the pictures. The only men they had in the pictures were drag queens or muscle guys, but not everybody is a drag queen or a muscle guy." Consequently, as far as this member was concerned, it was as if the group were not part of the parade, and therefore symbolically annihilated.

This rejection is experienced even more acutely when it is big-on-big, inflicted by another big men's faction, the Bears, a group of hairy, beefy, lumberjack-type men. Choosing to emphasize their hairiness rather than their bulk, the Bears marketed themselves as rugged and masculine men, who broke off from Girth & Mirth. Their activities include camping in the woods, an actual bear's natural habitat. They can be recognized by their working-class drag (cut-off flannel shirts and tight, faded jeans) and their "woof" greeting followed up with a bear hug. They make hairy appearance highly desirable, while rendering fatness less significant. In fact, Girth & Mirthers find it difficult to compete with the popularity of the muscle-Bear. The Bears ended up marketing themselves so well as "real men" that they evolved into quite a successful subculture, rescuing gay men from the reputation of being effeminate through powerful animal imagery (i.e., totemism).[39] This led to stratification, knocking Girth & Mirthers down the gay social-class ladder. Today, there appears to be soft antagonism between Girth & Mirthers and the Bears. In fact, because of the Bears' success, one gay big man was told in a chatroom that Girth & Mirth "should just disband and let the Bears do their thing because there's no reason to encourage large people."

Girth & Mirth members also reported feeling unwelcome at Bear events. They feel tolerated, though not fully accepted, by the Bears. As one big man pointed out, "It just seems as though we are being dismissed as non-existent." The same Girth & Mirther told me about a joint bowling event, where most of the Bears "just kept to themselves and had their own conversations and more or less tolerated the fact that any Girth & Mirthers were there; they wanted to bowl among themselves, instead of with us. It wasn't as comfortable as I think it could have been, had they included us." Likewise, he bemoaned the Bears' half-hearted attempt to include Girth & Mirthers, because it seemed so insincere.

I have been to two Bear club meetings, and at neither one did anybody come up and say, "Hi, how are you? My name is Joe. I'm glad you're here," or "Welcome! Let me introduce you to some other members." That didn't happen. They're a big group and their membership numbers in the hundreds, if not thousands, of associates because of their Bear Camp run. That just struck me as if they're not willing to reach out; so, why should I bother? Had I been a more hairy guy, in better shape without a belly, or just being big all over or something, I might have been more welcomed, you know, an "A-list Bear" or a "Trophy Bear," or whatever you want to call them. But I was not comfortable there.

Another big man shared the injury he experienced at the Bear booth at Gay Pride. While he himself believed that his physicality fit the bill, he was ignored and came away feeling snubbed:

> I was interested and I wanted to talk to 'em. I'm a big, hairy guy. This is who I think I am. The guys working the booth more or less blew me off. They weren't interested in me or answering my questions. I don't know if that colored my perception of the Bear community, but I just didn't feel welcomed. They didn't care who I was, or anything like that, though it could have been the people they had manning the booth that day.

That said, Girth & Mirthers still have more of an affinity with the Bears than they do with the wider gay community, feeling more at home in a Bear bar that accommodates their size than in a trendy gay bar. After all, they share a history that bonds them, Girth & Mirth being the parent group. They also have similar experiences and vantage points from being part of a subculture within the gay community.

Excluded from Gay Spaces

Dramaturgical sociology teaches that boundaries constrain the movement of individuals between different regions.[40] This brings to mind an example of discrimination against fat women in the heterosexual world. Years ago, I would pass by a dive bar on my way home from work. A mural on the outside of the building depicted a laughable group of big white hens. The accompanying caption said in bold red letters, "NO Fat Chicks Allowed!" In effect the sign dissuaded, if not prevented, fat women from entering a public drinking establishment. In this context, the sign degraded all women as "chicks" and singled out fat women for their failure to meet male expectations of an "ideal" woman's physique.

There are no overt signs at the entrance to gay facilities saying "NO Fat Queens Allowed!" However, the sentiment is most certainly implied by the design of the interior spaces of these bars or restaurants. Big men generally do encounter spaces and furniture in which they cannot fit. For example, one Girth & Mirther commented, "A lot of the bars are not built for big people. One of the dance clubs has those hallways and the little areas you have to move through, and it's almost impossible because you inevitably wind up with people trying to pass each other and when you have a big person trying to pass, it becomes an issue." From my field observations, I gathered that when Girth & Mirthers go out as a group to a nightclub, they find it difficult to move beyond the walls of Bear bars and dance clubs. In other gay spaces, they are not only emotionally snubbed, but they also feel physically excluded. It is easier for them to go out to a Bear bar or eat at a restaurant or a buffet in the mainstream community that accommodates big people.

According to Goffman, social actors create boundaries to control access to certain performances.[41] The sign "NO Fat Chicks Allowed!" (as well as the admission of the right kind of "thin" chicks) represents aggression toward all women. Therefore, the sign was not just controlling access and excluding fat women; it was telling thin women that, in order to qualify as "chicks," they had to fall under an unspecified weight. Thus, the sign was ambiguous enough to make it potentially dangerous for even a thin woman to enter. In essence, the sign implied that even a thin woman would be regarded as a particular kind of sex object (a degradable one)—and with that came the fear that she could be harmed for belonging to that category. Moreover, the sign informed passersby that a fat woman could not audition at this bar for the gender-role stereotype of "chick" without being rejected for her size.

Women who encounter the "NO Fat Chicks Allowed!" sign must grapple with exclusion and even a whole other issue of potential violence if they accept the terms of admission. Exclusionary front-entry designs like this, which categorize people and blatantly prohibit them from entering, serve as boundary-setting devices. They humiliate and force one to agree to an inferior status. Any woman of any weight who decides to enter an establishment that announces "NO Fat Chicks Allowed!" would have to check her self-respect at the door. Likewise, given the gay community's tacit agreement to shun big gay men, those who choose to enter a trendy gay establishment would have to mentally prepare to be brushed off and ignored.

The felt experience of everyday shame makes Girth & Mirthers even more sensitive to the social and bodily exclusion that plays out in architectural space, furniture design, and bathroom layout. Over Friday night coffee, the men of Girth & Mirth mentioned the offputting layout of a local gay bar and grill, the hub of the city's gay scene, that reopened at a new location. At the former location, where the Girth & Mirthers went for Sunday brunch, the bar had an open concept: movable, high round tables in the seating area with plenty of space to accommodate large gatherings. It had a spacious bathroom with a roomy, easily accessible stall. In contrast, they pointed out that the present location's narrow entrance ramp with a metal railing immediately makes them feel closed in. Inside, seats are crammed into the space, making it hard to navigate one's way through the crowd to an empty table, if there is one. The big men also said the new location has tiny bathrooms that evoke feelings of claustrophobia.

Some Girth & Mirthers speculated that the new design was a deliberate attempt to keep them out. One member summed it up by saying, "They don't want us there." While this architectural layout may be intentional, to help promote a hopping atmosphere, it makes it difficult for patrons to move around, especially for men of size. As one member so aptly put it, "Aside from lucking out and finding empty patio space, the new design cannot accommodate us big girls." Eventually, members started frequenting a mainstream restaurant that was more architecturally accommodating.

The big men's inability to fit into the space that the new bar offers transforms their ordinary activities into experiences of exclusion. This leads to everyday shame for big gay men. The taken-for-granted design of the bar and grill overlooks their needs and ultimately renders them invisible, despite their visibly large bodies. However, the big men do not want to be embarrassed in gay spaces for having special accommodations made for them, either, which would single them out as if to say, "FAT People Sit Here." Thus, the remedy for gay big men would be one of *accessibility without stigma*, rather than one of segregated inclusion. Big men would like to have accessible public spaces that do not call attention to them, even while including them.

Thus, Girth & Mirthers have found a fat-affirming space in the Bear bar where they host their charity fundraising nights. Intended for gay Bears, leathermen, and cowboys, this bar's interior differs from the remodeled gay bar and grill. Here, an oversized metal door accommodates guests, the bottom of the doorframe flush with the sidewalk and the parking lot out front. Within the wide-open space of the club, there is a large, often unoccupied dance floor. Lining the walls are two bars. Then there is a comfy seating area with an enormous couch and chairs, a few round bar tables, and sturdy metal stools. The roomy bathroom includes a king-sized stall with a custom-made, doublewide plywood door. A patio out back spans the length of the building, replete with a sturdy wooden bar, easy-to-move bistro tables, and a variety of seating, amounting to a gay big man's haven, which, instead of humiliating, welcomes him.

Grappling with Self-Loathing

It is difficult for gay big men not to internalize the shame they experience in mainstream society, and particularly within the gay community. One big man from Girth & Mirth described his daily struggle with being "overweight" as follows:

> There are days when I think I'm huge and there are days I *know* I'm huge.
> There are other days when I'm like, "I have a good job, I have a man who

loves me, I love him, I'm comfortable, I have everything I could possibly want or need." In the grand scheme of things, yeah, I'm 50 to 70 pounds overweight, but being overweight doesn't control my life. Then there are days I just can't look at myself in the mirror because I'm thinking, "My God, you're so hideous," and I turn the lights out [he chuckles].

While this big man said he tries to avoid letting his weight run his life, he readily admitted to self-loathing that sometimes drives him to turn out the lights so he will not have to see his fat body in the mirror. Despite his good situation and positive outlook most of the time, he still acknowledged that he is unable to overcome completely his internalized fatphobia.

Being in the company of Girth & Mirthers could be a double-edged sword. In some cases, it could be that, because misery loves company, some big men would want to indulge in self-deprecating "fat talk." However, it is more likely that Girth & Mirthers will help one another out by reframing their discouraging dialogue and negative thoughts. The environment and activities the club offers are conducive to overcoming fat negativity. The club engages them in normalizing activities like coming together for coffee, having a pot-luck, attending game night, enjoying a pool party, or going to the movies, out to dinner, or to brunch.

Big gay men often bemoan the fact that "fat" becomes an overriding category that overshadows their sexuality and denies that they are sexual beings. Ironically, about the only time they feel they are identified as "gay" first and foremost takes place within mainstream society, even as this acknowledgment is meted out in the form of harassment. In contrast, within the gay community, they are labeled as "fat" first, because of their failure to fulfill the gay ideal body type.

Simply recounting tales of abject defeat and humiliation or fat people's sob stories could amount to little more than making the empathetic reader feel good for the duration of the story. However, it is important to understand the particular nature of the various injuries inflicted on gay big men in order to appreciate the excessive lengths they go to in order to reconfigure their shame. The big men who participated in this study provided a laundry list of complaints of being harassed, shamed, brushed off, rendered invisible, profiled, bullied, excluded, and degraded. Out of this litany, it is those injuries which correspond with weight discrimination within the gay community that are the focus of this book. It is these injuries that cause gay big men to work so hard to repackage themselves boldly as human beings *and* as sexual beings who deserve to be part of a community and to experience the same pleasures other gay men do.

This is what Girth & Mirthers are all about: They nurture one another's joy in being fat and happy. What makes their everyday shame of being fat worthwhile is that they take the next step to reconfigure their being fat. Though they are constantly confronted with humiliation, they manage to sustain the integrity of their everyday lives by continuing to look for creative responses to the shame that comes with being fat and gay. Beyond individually internalizing shame, and beyond normalizing it with the help of fellow sufferers, big men launch bolder comebacks that range from sexualizing their hurts to reconfiguring their injuries and aestheticizing and performing their fat bodies unapologetically.

3

Performing the Fat Body

Every summer, Girth & Mirth holds a reunion together with other big men's clubs, allowing big gay men a safe and supportive environment in which they can have an opportunity to sexualize the injuries they experience in the gay world. In this sexed-up celebration of the chub/chaser community and culture, big gay men gather once a year at the Cabana Inn,[1] the largest gay resort in the Southwest, to party and to maintain ties with other big men from around the country, rekindle old friendships, and make new ones. Within the confines of this alternative space, they feel free to disrupt the categories of status and privilege based on body shape and size, by displaying their "goods" and acting out sexuality that has come to be "forbidden" to big men.

Being "big" tends to relegate big men to the status of sexual second-class citizens, for it is regarded as sexually undesirable, particularly in the gay community. Yet, sexuality is one of the essential markers of adult humanity; it connects human beings to one another. The Super Weekend is designed to meet this most basic of human needs. The injury big gay men experience is one of being perceived as "disgusting" and "sexually repulsive." In response to that injury, the big men construct and perform their fat bodies as objects of desire, at least for the duration of the Super

Weekend. And in the socially constructed space of campy spectacle and joyous carnival, they redefine themselves as sex objects: sexual beings who are motivated by the desire of other men.

The Super Weekend at the Cabana is a repetition of a safe space each year. It offers shelter from an increasingly normalized gay scene that seems to have become rather sterile. Oddly enough, however, it is held in Oklahoma, which is an inhospitable region of the United States for gays—not exactly the best shelter from homophobia. However, this hostile environment has concentrated the gay culture there into a rich and lively gay ghetto. For one short weekend reunion, the Cabana provides a fat-affirming sanctuary where big men need not be embarrassed, surrounded by other men like themselves and their admiring playmates.

The big men's over-the-top behavior at the reunion is a reaction to forms of dehumanization and desexualization that place them at a disadvantage to other gay men in the sexual marketplace. It is understandable that in so doing, big men are purposefully extreme, as they affirm the sex-object piece and give themselves and one another license to play and be naughty in ways they might not have the opportunity for as readily the rest of the year. This is one precious weekend in which big gay men can amp up their sexual selves and have the pleasure of transforming themselves into sex objects. Thus, the carnivalesque Super Weekend at the Cabana illustrates how big gay men highlight what has been missing in their lives, through displaying it to an excess, and how performing the fat body using the transgressive spirit of carnival assists in the mission of the weekend.

The two-story '60s-style motel set in Oklahoma City's "gayborhood" is a self-contained world with a restaurant, three bars, a gift shop, and rooms arranged in quadrangles around two pools. As they do every July, about 175 big men and their admirers from all over the nation descend upon the motel's pools for this devilishly fun Super Weekend. Several huddle in groups and talk, some relax along the water's edge, while others play with Styrofoam pool noodles. Most wear traditional swim trunks, a few parade around in thongs and Speedos, and one or two merely strip down to their underwear. For one weekend a year, campy water spectacles and splashy fun wash away the wounds of the homophobic and fatphobic derogatory messages these men battle daily.

It takes a lot of hard work to engineer a multigroup festival like this. Guests rave about the combined effort of the four different big men's groups that sponsor the event. The goal is to enable the guests to feel free to engage in behavior they would not dare undertake elsewhere, without the camaraderie this annual event fosters. The planned activities for the weekend support a kind of theatrical mode in which the guests feel accepted for who they are within the carnival setting, where time in one's everyday life is suspended. What makes a weekend ritual like this difficult to orchestrate is the added need for these performances of various supportive expressions to establish, rekindle, and maintain interpersonal relationships and group cohesion.[2]

The vibrant carnival and burlesque infrastructure of the Super Weekend gives big gay men an outlet for their desires, with less of the stigma. It enables them as part of a collective to put themselves "out there," something fierce, with a sense of humor and defiance. In the words of Bakhtin, this is "the feast of becoming, change, and renewal" which "celebrate[s] temporary liberation from the prevailing truth and from the established order; it mark[s] the suspension of all hierarchical rank, privileges, norms, and prohibitions."[3] The men enjoy exchanging witty barbs used affectionately both to "praise and abuse" and to "crown . . . and uncrown . . . " one another, all in one fell swoop.[4] Here, they are both undone and revitalized, as their suffering and fear are reduced, albeit temporarily.

At the Cabana once a year, the big men create an inverse world for themselves. For example, one year "chubs," as they like to refer to one another, lined up in the pool and spread their legs. Meanwhile, a handful of "chasers," or admirers with thinner builds who find big chubby men attractive, jumped in for the underwater swimming competition. The object of the game was for the chasers to swim across the pool and pass through the big men's legs, carefully dodging being leg-locked, with a few scrambling underwater to find their lost swim trunks. Chasers popped up at the end of the line one by one, as more chubs joined the fun. The chubs then instructed the chasers to kiss and make out for them. This aquatic sports parody and the makeout session among the chasers served to reverse roles, placing the chasers symbolically below the chubs.

Unlike in the larger gay community, the big men are encouraged at the Cabana to feel just as attractive as any gay man of "normal" size. Fat activist Marilyn Wann praises big gay men's "wonderful . . . extensive network[s]." She considers these men "freedom fighters, in the sense that living well is the best revenge":[5] partying, "getting laid," having a good time, big guys expressing sexuality and sensuality, just as other body types of gay men do. Chub/chaser networks and reunions such as the Super Weekend allow fat gay men to resist the belief that others could deny them such fun because of their weight and size.

My Researcher Position

After lunch on Thursday at the Cabana's restaurant, a group of big men who have arrived early for the weekend come out to bask in the comfort and freedom of campy-queer behavior and profane talk that are the order of the day. Chubby men spray on sunscreen as they get ready to relax in the hot sun. One of the men in the pool jokes that it looks as if they are greasing up with PAM cooking spray. As the pool fills with big men, the water overflows the rim. The spillover pushes their cocktails along the edge farther and farther out of reach, creating a topic of conversation. The flirty chubs take the opportunity to strike up deals with poolside folks to retrieve their out-of-reach drinks for them. One big man zeroes in on me, a new face, lounging poolside. He razzes me about my sunburn and slender build and calls me a "twink": "You need to eat a fried Twinkie, but you can't because that would be cannibalism." I flash a nervous smile and say nothing.

To the guests, I look like a chaser. But, because I am skirting this subject position, what else can they do with my size but use it to pick on me? If they cannot place me in the position of a chubby-chaser, and I am not out as a researcher, then the only option left is for them to perceive me as an aberration in my thinness.

This year, the Ohio Girth & Mirthers with whom I came are co-hosting the event, and I have been asked at the last minute to serve as one of the coordinators because one couple had to cancel as a result of an injury. My functional role as coordinator gives me the opportunity to gain a deeper understanding of what Super Weekends are all about. As a first-time coordinator and an inexperienced ethnographer, I am happy to keep busy.

The leaders of the Ohio Girth & Mirth group, my key informants and companions who graciously invited me, think it best for me not to go around advertising the fact that I am a researcher, as that knowledge might detract from the festivities. I have qualms about this suggestion. Despite all of my graduate training in research methods and reading about other people's researcher dilemmas, I never envisioned myself being in this position. The participants have a right to know that I am conducting a study. I knew I would be forgoing the use of signed consent forms while researching a large, public gathering such as this; but I had not necessarily planned on avoiding my researcher status altogether. I trust my key informants' insider knowledge and respect their agency. I courteously bow to their greater wisdom and comply with their wishes to keep my researcher role under wraps. The Super Weekenders who are on a moral holiday likely have identities they also will choose not to disclose.

Eventually, a group of us get out of the pool to have dinner before the coordinators' meeting and head up the stairs. One of the coordinators turns and asks me if I am feeling okay after being teased at the pool. I tell him I am fully aware that thinness is not necessarily a category of privilege in this setting and say, "I'm fine." I am, in fact, negotiating my position as ally-outsider-within.

Welcome Party at the Hospitality Suite

We are supposed to put together the Chub-and-Chaser Contest and sell raffle tickets for the 50/50 drawing. In the 50/50, a ticket is drawn at the close of the contest. The winner receives half of the ticket sales, and the host groups split the rest. As a coordinator, I am also expected to enforce the rule that no bottles or glassware enter the pool area, remind guests to close the curtains to their rooms while they are having sex, and alert security if hustlers cause any trouble on the premises. In addition, I am asked to do a couple of two-hour bartending shifts and make sure guests show their passes as they enter the hospitality suite.

My first bartending shift begins at noon on Friday. I start as a bar-back, the bartender's assistant, gradually taking over as he becomes tipsy. The bartender is a fun-loving, young-looking twenty-something, with a round face and oval-shaped glasses that accentuate his chubby cheeks. His body harness draws attention to his belly with a large center ring in the front fastened together by chunky black straps. He shows off his plump derrière in leather chaps and a Stars-and-Stripes jockstrap, reveal-ing, rather than camouflaging, his fat body.

Super Weekend guests come from all walks of life. Across the room is Bubbelz, a big and tall older dandy with a bouncy personality in a long lime polo shirt who graciously holds out his hand to the doorman for a kiss. I refill a young and beefy guy's white ceramic Buddha mug. His companion looks twice his age. The group I came with also picked up in Indianapolis a black bear cub—a hairy teddy bear with a braided rattail and dark scraggly beard, young and not that big. He is popular among these circles; he does stand-up comedy and works as a DJ at events like this. He has been slated to emcee the chub contest this year; but for now, he just hooks up his iPod to play music.

My second shift begins at six. I help to set up the hors d'oeuvres table for the welcome party, which takes on a distinctly carnivalesque atmo-sphere. Tex, who acts like the carnival showman, is an older super-chub who is all too used to the challenge of finding comfortable seating.

During my first shift, I saw Tex place a sturdy chair without arms at the entrance for the greeter. He told me his folding travel stool from the online shop Living XL has been a lifesaver for him. In the hospitality room, he monitors the rented "squishee" machine that mixes a popular carnival concession: frozen strawberry margaritas, a bright red slush that packs a Texas-sized punch. Tex volunteers to be one of the "waist or double-inseam" ticket sellers every year. He runs a good old-fashioned carny game reminiscent of the weight-guessing one at amusement parks. Tonight, the local leader of the Ohio chapter of Girth & Mirth is an apprentice to Tex. He is shirtless and wearing a carnival costume of crotchless suspender shorts. He is "going commando," letting it all hang out.

There are two ways to be fitted for raffle tickets, both of which cost the same. The first uses ticket tape to measure the buyer or, if the buyer prefers, the seller's waist. A variation on this theme, "waist of your choice," was discontinued this year, as it was awkward for the largest guest. NOLOSE (previously the National Organization for Lesbians of Size) also did body wraps at one of its Big Fat Queer Proms and sold tickets by waist or bust measurement.[6] Carnival stunts like this, thoughtfully performed, signify an advantage to being big, wherein the greater the girth, the more tickets the buyer can get, and the greater the odds he will be a winner. The second way of being fitted for raffle tickets is called "the double inseam." The seller takes inseam measurements by running the ticket tape up the buyer's trouser leg, across his crotch, and down to his other ankle. The trick is that the seller also loops the ticket tape around the buyer's scrotum.

Tex performs a special double inseam for a shy first-time visitor. In his deep voice with a southern drawl, he gives his opening schtick on getting fitted for tickets; his sidekick reassures the buyer that Tex can retract the tape without causing any paper cuts. Up the guest's pants he goes, stopping to rub the blushing man's penis and giving a carnival callout to the others in the room, "I think we've got a wiener!" After he pulls out the tickets, he holds them up and says, "I bet you didn't know your inseam was this long." The secret is, with a sleight-of-hand, everyone gets about the same number of tickets.

Mardi Gras closes out the final hours of the welcome party—the most elaborate event in the hospitality suite. A short and fat old man in leopard-print underwear asks me for a diet soda, parks his motorized wheelchair by the bar, then sits back to take in the festivities. By now, the bartender who worked with me earlier has returned to replace me. He brought in strings of party beads for us to detangle before I go. This time, he came in shirtless, wearing white football pants, his black rubber jockstrap visible through skintight spandex, with a label on the center of it that reads, "Nasty Pig." He boasts his athletic uniform and playgear of chaps and jockstrap as if to say, "I am a real pig who likes it dirty."

Here in the carnival-like atmosphere, fat exhibitionism like this is welcome and supported. As one of the Midwest coordinators and co-emcee for the contest told me earlier, "At the Super Weekend, you can feel attractive. Three hundred sixty-two days a year, people make jokes about you, but here you can go into the pool and an admirer may say, 'Look at that fat guy,' as a compliment." These remarks remind me of how, at similar big men's events, the doorman announces each guest's arrival by saying, "Hot man coming in!"

Friday Evening Falls over the Cabana

The lighted pool shimmers by night, though its crystal-clear cerulean-blue water will soon turn cloudy. The influx of guests slathered with tanning oil fouls up the pool's filtration system. Plus, a few locals who just bought daily passes for the weekend, as well as renters and those gay transients tolerated by the motel, have come to have fun at the pool with the big men, free of charge. The numbers quickly add up and the pool's filtration system can no longer keep up.

At night, most of the men lounge around the pool and carry on quiet conversations. A stick-thin local dangles his legs in the pool. Tan, with peroxide-blond hair spiked with gel, this young man rarely gets into the water the entire weekend but flirts with the big men alongside the edge. Tonight, the three chubs who linger in the pool gather around his legs like a trio of dolphins. They bob close to the pool's rim, their heads just above the water's surface, their bodies lit up indistinctly below.

Past the concrete walkway around the pool is an arbor bench that makes a good poolside cabana. Sitting there is a shy Cherokee super-chub, talking to his friends. I take a seat next to him on a chaise longue. He rubs my bald head, *my* source of body anxiety; he asks if everybody does that to me and if the men here hit on me. The lucky fellow himself has a full head of thick chin-length black hair. He says he goes to a Cherokee Baptist church and two weeks ago, he ventured off to a Two-Spirit meeting. He works outside of Tulsa doing Cherokee family services. Over the weekend, his friends have taken to calling him "Pocahontas." G.W., a short fat man, is full of life as he sashays around the pool in a silver wrestling singlet. He says he owns a chain of salons. As he passes by, he tries to draw out Pocahontas, saying to me in his honey-dipped Carolina accent, "She's been in that same spot all night workin' it, her best angles and poses." Both of these men have been to this event before.

I leave the poolside and meander in the direction of my room. Each room at the inn has a large picture window as in Amsterdam's red light district. A hot-pink sign in the window designates a coordinator's room. Others tape up club banners to their windows. I am told that one year, a group hung the club's Pride parade banner over the upstairs balcony railing, and behind it, they put plastic flamingos in the window.

I also learned that there used to be a carnivalesque window-dressing contest. The motel, well known for balcony bingo—a type of gay cruising or voyeurism wherein men stroll by different room numbers in search of chance encounters—ironically shut down one window for being too provocative.[7] As I was told, the label on the window read, "Peepshow." The lodgers had covered it in black paper and cut out a faux glory hole, resembling an opening designed for anonymous oral sex. When people walking by looked through the peephole, they saw yellow marshmallow Peeps, the kind parents put in their children's Easter baskets. This peepshow window suggests that carnival is *more* than just show; as with the raffle ticket sales, it requires viewers' active participation. However, from the motel's perspective, the peepshow window sends the wrong message. Most other guests simply decorate their windows with paint or kitschy items arranged on the ledge, such as twinkly lights, inflatable dolls, stuffed animals, or their club banners, with some selections more humorous than others.

When I unlock the door to my room, my roommate, another coordinator, stirs in his sleep. Last year, he was unhappy with his room because it was too close to the scat room where sex play involving feces went on. This year, he has been up, off and on throughout the night, to answer salacious phone calls and drunken dialers. Coordinators are required to leave their phones on all night. Guests' phone numbers correspond with their room numbers; and though most calls are random, the guys do know how to dial up those men they are pursuing. Last night, someone kept calling our room saying nothing, but breathing heavily; by 4:00 A.M., he had drummed up the courage to talk dirty. Tonight, I answer the phone and tell my roommate jokingly that the call is for him. He rolls over, talks to the caller, and then tells me the man on the line wanted to know if we would like to buy some porn.

The Morning After

An all-you-can-eat breakfast buffet runs from 9:00 to 11:00 at the Copa, the hottest spot on the north side of the Cabana. Raffle tickets are still on sale at the club entrance. This Vegas-style Egyptian-themed dance club hosts drag and strip shows. On weekends like this throughout the year, the Copa becomes home to various special events.

Another coordinator and I get some food, sit at a table, and talk with an elderly gay man from Kansas. He tells us he belongs to a group for older gay men, the Wichita Prime Timers, and sometimes goes to its holiday events. However, he says the gay men there act too old for his taste and he disidentifies with them. The Prime Timers, founded in Boston circa 1987 by a retired professor, Woody Baldwin, are organized around old age in the same way Girth & Mirthers are organized around ample size. Both clubs show compassion for underdogs in gay society, and both work hard to draw out folks who may live in social isolation. This man, though, suggests that the Prime Timers narrowly disrupt normative understandings of what it means to be gay and getting on in years. In fact, their brochure in the motel lobby talks about how older gay men prefer friendships with mature men their own age, which underscores his concern. This is why he is drawn to the Super Weekend at the Cabana, where gay men of all ages and sizes can play sexually if they like, reveling in an earthy, crass sense of humor that helps to keep them young.

Last year's winner of the Mr. Chaser contest, a handsome school-teacher who lives in a French-German border town, comes to join us for breakfast. He is a short, barrel-chested, blond and blue-eyed athletic type in his thirties who likes to show off his tan body in a snug-fitting white swimsuit. He tells us he goes to many of these events, as well as Bear runs during his summer holidays. Last weekend, he went to the Bear Camp in Ohio, where the guys roped him into a lube-wrestling match. When the other coordinator asks him if he is going to be in the chaser half of the contest this year, he says he has decided not to enter again, as he does not want to run the risk of losing his title.

This soon-to-be-former Mr. Chaser tells us about his sexual exploits. He says he slept with a really big guy the previous night. When he woke up this morning, the man was lying asleep on his arm. He then proceeds to show us a huge bruise on his muscular forearm, as though it were a badge of honor, a souvenir of his sexual encounter with a chub. By day two, it is possible to tell this kind of war story around the breakfast table, but it disturbs me nonetheless, because of his "damned desire," and too much of it. There is a strong taboo against a gay man with the "ideal" body type like his pairing up with a super-chub when he could attract a whole host of sexually "appropriate" partners. While he is able to indulge in this "inappropriate" choice of sex partner within this inverse world, he *cannot* let himself admit that the sex was good. So, he dwells on the

bruise he suffered. This bruise not only speaks volumes about his preoc-
cupation with big men but also seems to symbolize his fierce resistance
to a thwarted sexual desire. Perhaps the truth is he likes this kind of sex,
getting crushed under a big body on top of him, and he enjoys displaying
the bruise as evidence of the previous night's pleasure.

The Chub-and-Chaser Contest

Around two o'clock, I stand in line with Pocahontas at the Copa for the
"Texas-Sized All-You-Can-Eat Bar-B-Que." Pocahontas teases me and
claims he told the ticket seller he wanted to buy my teeny waist size
in tickets, which would amount to merely two. The barbecue makes
me smile, thinking back to a tale I heard last spring at a kaffeeklatsch
about a prior year's carnival performance called the "K.C. Masterpiece."
K.C. was described to me as being a "big dirty loudmouth." At one of
the banquets, they said, K.C. got up on stage, rubbed barbecue sauce
all over his stomach, then danced around and lifted his flabby belly up
over the railing. The servers and audience members at the back of the
room gasped in horror—from afar, it looked as though he were fecal-
smearing. I was told that for many folks there, tongue-in-cheek, it made
for an unsavory banquet. Since then, to prevent mishaps on stage, the
contest information form states, "NOTICE: The use of any hidden props,
toys or condiments will be cause for immediate disqualification from
the contest."

Organizing the Contest

Before the contest begins, the coordinators all stand in front of the stage
and throw out large shirts, hats, and other donated goodies to the audience. The organizers of the show tell us not to toss the items just to our
friends. I go ahead, though, and throw a Girth & Mirth logo tee and ball-
cap to a couple whom I met over the weekend. I also try to fling a shirt
to Pocahontas, but he is sitting too far away and it ends up falling short.

After the toss-outs comes the chaser portion of the contest. The chub bit is supposed to follow the same format, which mocks a traditional beauty pageant. Typically, the ratio is off: More chubs than chasers enter the annual show. At a planning meeting, an organizer explained that chasers go first: "You get the small part out of the way like in show business and save the biggest and best contestants for last."

There are three parts to both the chub and the chaser contests: the interview, the question, and the fantasy dance show. The interview begins with a personal introduction of each contestant from his fact sheet. The organizers were thoughtful when they planned this sheet out and omitted occupation because they knew some folks would be on disability. The emcee banters with each person one by one in the lineup, embellishing their entry forms and giving the audience some juicy tidbits about them. The goal is to avoid taking the limelight off the entrants on stage.

On the contest information form, the entrants are instructed to "Feel free to be creative and fun. That's what this is all about." At the same time, as one organizer pointed out at last month's meeting, "Just because it's informal doesn't mean it has to look informal." This is a pseudo-contest; but it is well organized, aims to be drama-free, and moves along quickly. The form prompts the contestants to fill in their name; address; age; relationship status; chub or chaser; top, bottom, or versatile; favorite food and drink; and how their friends would describe them. At the end of the form is a "Help us get to know you better" section that asks the contestants to select one word from each list.

1. Bedroom, Backroom, Bathhouse, Patio, Hot Tub, Kiddies' Pool
2. Car, Convertible, Pickup Truck, Semi-Truck, SUV, Mini-Van
3. Blue jeans, Chinos, Shorts, Kilts, Drag, Leather, Uniform
4. Boxers, Briefs, Boxer-Briefs, Thongs, Jockstraps, Commando

The emcee uses the information from this form to introduce each contestant, while sexualizing his word choices—all in good fun. When the introductions are over, the contestants exit stage right.

Then, one by one, the contestants reemerge on stage, some shirtless, some in skimpy attire, and a few in various uniforms, to answer a fantasy scenario question. It was the Ohio Girth & Mirthers who prepared the list of questions, ranging from fun and entertaining to scandalous, like "What was the worst or most successful pick-up line you've ever heard?" After answering a question, each contestant joins the other men in a lineup onstage, and they all prance around. On the whole, the big men on the stage and in the audience do not take themselves too seriously, which permits fat and gay fun to spill out all over the place. On stage and off, the contest is driven by play.

The chub and the chaser contests both conclude with a contestant dance-off, often with their pants off, where the guys get to strut their stuff. The audience then votes for a winner by applause. As it was explained to me, "It appears as if there are judges, but really it's the audience who decides. With applause, the benefit is you instantly know who the winner is, whereas with votes, you have to waste time tallying them." Like the peepshow window and the raffle ticket sales, the Chub-and-Chaser Contest is a carnival that relies on an actively engaged, lively audience. Indeed, true to Bakhtin's depiction of carnival, this is "a pageant without footlights and without a division into performers and spectators."[8] The Super Weekend fosters participatory spectacles that, in the case of the Chub-and-Chaser Contest, break down the boundaries between the contestants and the audience.

The Dance of the Chasers

Six chasers are in the contest this year. Contestant number one has the painted face of Quentin Crisp and walks out on stage like a beauty queen in a pair of leopard-print trunks. When the emcee asked him earlier, "What cartoon character would you have sex with?" he replied, "Dennis the Menace." The audience looked puzzled, but at least he managed to give a tight-lipped smile, plus he shot the crowd a thumbs-up.

Entrant number two is the guy who bartended with me. He comes out in a metallic-blue wrestling singlet and boots. A few folks in the audience say he is too big to be in the chaser contest; later on, they gripe about two older men, entrants four and five, being too big. Number three, though, fits the bill, with his shaved head, goatee, tattoos, and piercings; he exudes *über*-masculinity and swaggers onto the stage with his hands in his pockets, his "camo" cargo shorts sagging on his lanky frame.

The last chaser, Devanté from the Hoosier state, lets loose over the course of the show and breaks out into erotic dance moves. He is a young and "average-looking" black man who knows how to work the audience. He rolls up his t-shirt sleeves to show off his toned arms. The front of his shirt reads, "THE BACK VIEW IS EVEN BETTER!" and the back reads, "THE FRONT VIEW IS EVEN BETTER!" The high-cut V-shaped thong he is wearing gives him long, shapely legs and exposes his round behind.

With Devanté in the lead, the six men flaunt their stuff. My fellow bartender pulls down the shoulder straps on his singlet. Devanté moves center stage and puts his leg up on the railing. The guy in the army print shorts hangs back, drops his drawers, and moons the audience. Upping the ante, Devanté strips his shirt off and all eyes are on him. I can now see that his thong has a zipper in the front with a ring pull. He begins to do a pole dance: The other people on stage laugh and smile as he humps a column. One of the big older men gets near the stage railing right beside him, turns his back to the audience, and moons them. Devanté and the man in the camo cargo shorts continue to play off of each other: The latter moons the audience again; the former puts his shirt back on, does the splits, and runs his fingers through his hair.

As the song-and-dance routine winds down, the audience is howling with laughter. They clap while the emcee stands beside each contestant and calls out their names. The emcees and organizers work together around the room and determine that the audience applause-o-meter has it down to two people: Devanté and his challenger in camo shorts, the one who oozed sexual prowess. The emcee again asks for applause to determine who the winner is, and it is Devanté, hands down. Meanwhile, the incoming emcee brings out the trophy and presents it to Devanté. It is a stately glass trophy that has the simple silhouette of a chub and a chaser etched on it, designed by an artist from the Ohio Girth & Mirth group. The photographer, who likes to travel to all chub-and-chaser events around North America and Europe to record them, asks Devanté to hold up his trophy and smile.

The Doorknob Award

At halftime, the audience picks out who ought to win the Doorknob Award. Other formal organizations also give out this award to members who have opened up their doors to let in new folks. The Doorknob, in the hypersexual context of the Super Weekend, is a mock award. It humorously recognizes the guest who has contributed the most to helping others acculturate to the group through his undying efforts to have sex with every man there. One of the event planners described it like this: "Traditionally, it has to do with a vote based on the number of sexual partners a guest has had over the weekend; or the award is won by acclamation—ergo, it's a drunkard award."

As Sontag notes, Oscar Wilde celebrated "the equivalence of all objects." Foreshadowing one of the joys of camp, or its "democratic *esprit*," Wilde said that anything, even a doorknob, can be elevated to the status of "fine" art if one views it through the lens of a camp sensibility.[9] Thus, in the campy setting of the Super Weekend, the annual winner of the Doorknob for best sexual performance literally receives a doorknob. This year, the Doorknob Award consists of a white wooden star trimmed in red with a crystal doorknob mounted to the center of it. It was custom-made by a retired architect from the Ohio Girth & Mirth group. The base of the award has a plaque that reads, "DOORKNOB AWARD" and has a talking "Easy" button on it from a Staples office supplies store. When the button is pressed, a mechanical male voice says, "That Was Easy!" as if the winner had it in the bag. In this inverse world, a crystal doorknob equals a golden trophy, and, as in the "real" world, men are rewarded by their buddies for engaging in casual sex.

This year, the emcee helps the audience narrow down the potential winners. He asks for a show of hands to indicate how many people have had sex with at least one person since they have been there. He shouts out, "Two? Three? More than five?" and so on. The nosy audience looks around with prurient interest to see whose hands are still going up.

This year, a big guy named Jackie wins the Doorknob Award and from what I hear, he has been winning it every year. He is an older man with a puffy face, baby-blue eyes, and a cheerful demeanor, and he has served as a longtime coordinator. His claim to fame is his sex stunts in semi-public places. I remember his telling a group of us walking by his room shortly after we arrived on Thursday that he already had sex with thirteen to fourteen people. As we stood outside his door, he attached a suction-cup dildo to it. Throughout the weekend, young men would enter his room, he would close the blinds, and then open them up again, repeating the routine with each new encounter.

At the welcome party in the hospitality room, Jackie pushed one man's legs up over his head on the couch and went down on him as if to give him a blowjob. Later, I remember seeing him messing around with this person's partner in front of the window, so that they had to close the blinds. Now, having thoroughly earned his award, he proudly holds it up for the photographer; then the coordinators come up to the front again, to do more toss-outs. I throw a Girth & Mirth tee and hat to a friend of Bubbelz's and head back to my seat for the chub contest.

Here Come the Chubs

The chub contestants wait in the corridor outside the club with a "fluffer" whose task it is to prepare the guys backstage and warm up the audience for them. He leads the crowd in a rousing chant and tries to get them riled up for the chubs. As these entrants walk in behind him, they stomp their feet, while he claps his hands over his head and leads the crowd in a cheer: "HERE-COME-THE-CHUBS,

HERE-COME-THE-CHUBS!"—synchronized to the rhythm of [clap, stomp] [clap, stomp] [clap, stomp] [clap, stomp].

Nine chubs are competing in the contest this year. "B.J. Boi,"[10] or as some have taken to calling him, "Cotton Candy," is contestant number one. He appears young, acts femme; he sashays onto the stage wearing a tight shirt with black- and see-through vertical bands that give the audience a peek at his chest and midsection—the parts of the body fat that gay males typically are most self-conscious about. B.J. Boi is unique in his choice of a femme persona, as most of the contestants construct a masculine persona on stage. Throughout the contest, for example, when asked, "What is your favorite food?" the men usually went with the male-identified food group—meat, or for a laugh, they threatened to eat chasers!

I look at all the masculine archetypes put forth on stage as fantasy fodder—some comical, as they try to live up to these unrealistic stereotypes. Number four, short and stout, comes out wearing a Harley Davidson cap and a flannel workshirt with cutoff sleeves. He selects "semi-truck" from the "get-to-know-you-better" list and jokes around about trolling truck-stop restrooms for chance encounters. Number five has a shaved head and a tattoo. He draws on his military background as he boasts of having fought in Desert Storm and says he had sex with nine guys in a foxhole. The sixth contestant has decided on a football player persona. He is a bearded man wearing a Denver Broncos jersey. Number seven's muscle shirt says it all: "Bears = Great Head." Contestant eight, a stocky silver daddy with rosy cheeks that make him resemble Ernest Hemingway, looks comfortable in his tie-dyed shirt. This daddy bear is met with shouts of approval from the audience: "Woof, woof!"[11] Suavely, he plants a kiss on the emcee's lips.

A young Hispanic newcomer is the final contestant. He comes out wearing crucifixes, denim shorts, and sandals. In response to the emcee's question about having sex with a cartoon character, he opts for "Casper the Friendly Ghost, because he can sneak in and sneak out." He then announces to the audience this is his first Super Weekend. He says he is really enjoying himself and appreciates that everyone has made him feel welcome. This contestant, feeling welcome at the Super Weekend, reminds me of the guy who sat alone reading at breakfast. A coordinator came and stood by him and dramatically waved the guy's copy of the latest Harry Potter book while calling out to the rest of the room how bored this guy must be to resort to this. He then asked everyone in the room to "Please make our guests feel welcome."

The emcee introducing the dance-off competition chides, "There will be no more doing the splits for the remainder of the contest. But if any of you chubs can do it, go ahead, and we'll get a shoehorn to pop you off the floor." Chubs take off their shirts and dance to the tune of "Hot Boyz"; they give it all they've got. Rolling his shirt up into a crop-top, B.J. Boi flag-dances using the black scarf wrapped around his shoulders, waving and spinning it to the music's rhythm. In a white jockstrap, the Desert Storm guy flicks his tongue à la Gene Simmons. The Denver Broncos contestant is swirling like a diva, cupping his breasts, dropping his drawers, and shaking his behind. The contestant who mentioned Casper the Friendly Ghost has quickly done a costume change: His leather body harness reveals the nipple piercings and tattoos on his chest, topped off with a Stetson hat and rainbow Pride bracelets. The contestant who referred to truck-stop restrooms coolly lowers his boxer shorts and bounces his ample buttocks up against the stage railing, and the crowd goes wild and cheers louder and louder. As the music fades, the emcee comes back onstage and invites the audience to vote for the best performer by applause. The crowd roots for the "Trucker"; his "total chub package" has won him the award.

It is now time for the raffle drawing. Some of the prizes include a registration package for another big men's weekend coming up the next month, a big men's porn video by Juggernaut XL Productions, a CD player, toy helicopters, and the big cash prize. I hear B.J. Boi, who has returned to a seat near me, question the fairness of the raffle when one of the ticket sellers wins both the $890 cash prize and the CD player. Most people, however, are happy for the winner, who in fact generously treats a large group of us to "the last supper" the following night.

My Researcher Dilemma

After the contest, I get into the pool, where I see B.J. Boi sauntering around the edge. He is wearing a rainbow horizontal-striped caftan, which he bought from Clovis, one of the founders of the Super Weekend, who is now in his eighties. For years, Clovis has been supplying these big gay men with his affordable, colorful clothing creations in extended sizes out of his makeshift store in the motel room next to his. The pool soon fills up with energized guests coming off the contest, cocktails in hand. Having recently read Bakhtin, I should have anticipated what happens next in a carnival setting like this—where "free and familiar contact among people"[12] is the norm and where taverns and bathhouses and the like are ideal contact zones.[13] As if fulfilling this formula, I am swarmed by three super-chubs, Roy, Pocahontas briefly, and G.W., who "cockblocks" Roy, trying to outmaneuver him from romantically pursuing me. Already inebriated, Roy makes a move on me, which I redirect by giving him a friendly hug, and he settles for a peck on my cheek. I am uncomfortable being the target of these advances both because I am here as a researcher and because I am in a committed relationship. I am also concerned about the waves the divers are making, because I cannot swim. Across the pool, one couple, whom I made friends with and who were in the know about my researcher status, jokingly suggest I shoot off a flare to call for help.

G.W. has had gastric bypass and he no longer gets hunger pangs, so his lover comes by to remind him to eat.[14] He explores his prospects with me by pointing out that I do not strike him as the "chaser" type. When I reply that size is not an issue for me, he feels encouraged to keep trying. So I say, "I have to go pee," and he playfully backs away from me. As I move toward the ladder, he offers me the key to his room, which he says is closer to the pool. I graciously decline and head to my room to regroup. When I return to the pool, I give G.W. the answer he will accept: "I have a boyfriend and we don't 'play.'"[15] By this point, G.W.'s lover is back, urging him to eat, and we part on friendly terms.

Later that evening at the motel's piano bar, I encounter a local gay man who wandered in to have a vodka tonic. He asks the bartender if the Super Weekend guys come into the bar. The bartender says, "No, not really," to which the guy comes back with a sexual innuendo: "Oh, it's not dirty enough for them?" Even though the bartender does not acknowledge the Super Weekend guests' sexuality, his noble explanation provides a caring challenge of the patron's attempt to disparage them: "They're good guys," he says. "They enjoy eating, but they are not big drinkers." The local quiets down, and, for now, an inflammatory tension has been defused. Herein lies the dilemma in which fat people's identities are bifurcated. The local hypersexualizes them, while the bartender mutes their sexuality.

The Wrap-Up Meeting

On the last day, having slept in, I go for lunch at Gusher's Restaurant by myself. It has floor-to-ceiling windows overlooking the pool. The restaurant's name was lost on me at first. This is, indeed, doubly "gusher" territory, with all this sexual release happening near the oil fields. From where I sit, I see an African American guest in a power wheelchair, stuck in the doorway to his room, with three men trailing behind him, who maneuver his wheelchair into the room and shut the door. I also see a chaser with bleached-blond hair and a thin, tan body fluffing up the big men around the pool, particularly the man from the contest with the Desert Storm persona. He takes a squirt gun and sprays the men. One of them in turn takes the squirt gun from him and wets down his white boxer briefs. I remember a story the men like to tell of a past Super Weekend when a big guy lying by the side of the pool was presumed dead because he was not moving. When a chaser walked by, the big guy's hand slowly rose into the chaser's trunks as everyone cheered, "He's alive! He's still reaching for dick!"

After lunch, I walk to the hospitality room with three of the coordinators and friends of theirs, as well as the couple I had befriended earlier.

We walk by the "twink pool"—this is "the other pool," where men who are part of the local gay scene hang out. The joke among the Super Weekend guests is that all the big guys ought to cannonball into the pool, sending the little "twinks" up into the trees. I am reminded once more that the pool is not always an equalizer; it is also the site where body shape and size are contested.

At the wrap-up meeting, among other things, we toy around with the idea that we ought to design a lifetime achievement award for Jackie, who has been winning the Doorknob Award every year. Then we consider creating more categories, because the chaser contest had as entrants chubs who liked chasing after other chubs. But we can see no end to category creation: There are chubby chubby-chasers, chub-for-chubs, or tweeners, whose body types do not fit either chub or chaser. Finally, we remark on the chaser emcee's behavior throughout the contest, which, at times, slipped into being mean-spirited. We note how he tried to steal the spotlight from the contestants, and some of his jokes were not even funny. This brought the organizers to a serious discussion about the responsibility of hosting an event like this with respect and compassion for the guests.

Redefining Fat through Carnival, Camp, and Play

The Pan–Girth & Mirth event is a pow-wow intended to put the big men at ease so they can socialize and find ways to play with definitions of their sexuality through camp and carnival. The Girth & Mirthers appear to use carnival as their resistance strategy against stigma; by Fabio Cleto's definition, camp is a "survivalist strategy."[16] The big men also use adult play to relate to one another. Their games range from unselfconsciously splashing around in a swimming pool, to sexually objectifying one another by acting out fantasies and role-playing in a safe environment.

The Super Weekend at the Cabana provides rich data for studying display culture among Girth & Mirth groups, organized around playfully sexualizing the injuries big gay men experience. Over the weekend, carnival performances are part of the commentary that constitutes the groups' culturally articulated categories that work on multiple levels. From the perspective of symbolic interactionists, and particularly among ethnomethodologists, people assess their own practices and behaviors. For example, the performances in the big men's mock beauty contest take on multiple meanings. They are a means of both social organization and of social critique. The manipulation of meaning on multiple levels represents the foundation of embodied or symbolic interaction. In this way, the big men's performance of their fat bodies carries sociological import.

It is difficult to produce an event such as the Super Weekend, in that it takes on a life of its own. It is a weekend of invention, in which both the organizers and the guests are creating the games, awards, and costumes. Once the idea of giving out a particular award occurs to the organizers one year, they are bound to come up with other categories the following year. Likewise, once the guests get a taste of how parading around in a suggestive outfit is received one year, they plan out their outfits even more carefully the next year.

The Super Weekend empowers its guests by providing an environment that gives them permission to display their goods, regardless, and perhaps precisely because, of their body shape and size. Because it is unsanctioned for fat bodies to show skin and wear seductive clothing, and because big men are not allowed to flaunt their bodies, they don various outfits as their weapon for "freedom fighting"[17] to combat desexualization and to achieve "temporary liberation"[18] from the sizist politics of fashion.

In picking out their wardrobes for the weekend, the big men engage in reinventing themselves as objects of desire and reclaiming their right to self-definition. I witnessed how difficult it was for one of the Super Weekend organizers to narrow down what to pack for the occasion. I was with him as he carefully considered his slogan tees neatly stored in bins under his bed. Some of the tees celebrated being big, such as

"Big Daddy," "Bigger Is Better," and "Big Dog's Well-Hung Drywall Co., We Have Big Tools!" He pulled out tees with funny/offensive slogans; some had double-entendres like the one that said, "Let's play army. I'll lie down and you can blow the hell out of me." Another tee displayed a screen-printed fire extinguisher holding its own nozzle to put out a fire, and the slogan read, "I put out." Yet another T-shirt had a grizzly bear on it with a slogan saying, "Come any closer, and I'll eat you up." Big men's sublimated sexuality surfaces when they dress to excess and play around with fashion. In so doing, they distinguish themselves from the image of big men as undifferentiated "slovenly fat slobs"; they redefine their size as something special, something with sexual currency. With the various tee slogans and evocative attire, these big men insinuate, tongue-in-cheek, that being big gives them bigger genitalia, rendering their sexuality larger than life.

In this type of fat-affirming performance frame, the meaning of dress changes; the big men's carefully selected adornment shows a rebellious attitude and serves a political function. Their fat-revealing, sexually suggestive clothing enables them to reframe their self-image within the carnivalesque infrastructure. The big men's clothing choices accentuate their fat bodies rather than camouflage them. Such exhibitionism is made possible by the carnival-like atmosphere, which gives guests license to be sexy and desirable. However, this exercise of power and celebration of one's fat identity takes place and remains within the safety and protection of the cohesive network of Girth & Mirthers. It does not reach mainstream society or the gay community, both of which normatively regulate and impose rigid ideals on the body.

Every year, guests purge themselves of their injuries by engaging in outrageous acts and pushing the limits. However, the limits seem to keep moving, because behavior that is intended to have shock value does not faze most of the guests. For example, when the big men playfully cause the chasers to lose their trunks in the swimming pool à la Janet Jackson's "nipple slip,"[19] their campy self-expression is, by definition, *intentionally* in bad taste, even as it results in a supposedly accidental indecent exposure. Such staged costume malfunctions force onlookers to feign shock, rather than really *be* shocked.

While the organizers and motel management appear to support testing the limits regarding the body and sexuality over the Super Weekend, they also impose limits when someone goes too far. For example, condiments were prohibited on stage after K.C. smeared barbecue sauce all over his body.[20] K.C.'s barbecue-sauce masterpiece was about magnifying rather than muting his shame surrounding food and fat, as if he were saying, "You think I am repulsive? Let me show you just how raunchy and disgusting I can be!" Like K.C., the Girth & Mirthers use carnival and camp to push the envelope as far as they can in their mission to resist stigma. By unapologetically engaging in "revolting" campy behavior, they thumb their noses at social sanctions against "obesity," thus appropriating power. Nevertheless, even at the Cabana, rules and regulations that try to restrict the big men replicate the limits one finds in the larger society. But with the safety net of the Super Weekend in place, limits are set without casting the big men into a marginal position among "normals" and "ideal" gays. At least the restrictions are imposed within the context of this time and place, in which the big men are among their own.

The big men's carnival acts that go well beyond all prohibitions at the Super Weekend would be frowned upon if carried out elsewhere. But as a group, they have a good time engaging in scatological humor and have fun celebrating outrageous and grotesque bodily expressions that center on things like food, fat, and sex. Bakhtin says of carnival gatherings: "[T]he body and bodily life have here a cosmic and at the same time all-people's character."[21] With their slum-like qualities, carnivals offer something special. As Bakhtin so eloquently puts it, "Behind all the slum-naturalism . . . , the carnival square is glimmering."[22] Indeed, the over-the-top antics at the Cabana are cosmic *and* ordinary. The Super Weekend is literally marvelous in its deviance while at the same time so very down to earth.

In the inverse world of the Super Weekend, the big men can negotiate the gay hierarchy through play. Carnival offers chubs the possibility to reconfigure and reframe the power dynamics, so that they can make the chasers submit sexually. Now, it is the chubs, rather than men with "ideal" physiques, who have a chance to call the shots. The big men perform their fat bodies unapologetically, and their body talk enables them to reject the socially sanctioned ideal of the thin gay man. In this context, categories of status and privilege based on body shape and size are temporarily disrupted. Thus, the roles are reversed; now it is the thin guests in the minority, and they become the potential targets of good-natured teasing and heckling. Such a reversal is unlikely to occur in the wider gay community with its beauty hierarchy, which rewards the svelte muscular figure.

Within the safe confines of the Cabana, big men seek sexual objectification to learn how to be open to and accepting of, and relate intimately to, one another, as in the sheltering idea from Goffman's book *Stigma*.[23] This is a diverse group that allows chubs and chasers, in the free, familiar setting of a swimming pool, to gather on an almost equal footing and feel "sexy." One big man shared with me: "When you're at the pool and everybody is more or less of the same build, then you are more likely to be comfortable with yourself, taking your shirt off and getting in the pool." The Super Weekend is about the critical role of multiple expressions of intimacy that reawaken big men's dormant sexuality. Unencumbered by social norms, many big men who have become detached from their bodies have the chance here to get reacquainted with them.

At the Cabana, "together unselfconsciously,"[24] the big men seem to be at ease with their bodies. Here, they are able to let go of the yardstick against which they have become accustomed to measuring themselves. In Gloria Steinem's terms, their "diverse reality wear[s] away the plastic-stereotypical-perfect image."[25] She explains how that perfect image "has worn a groove in our brains. It will take the constant intimacy of many new images to blast us out."[26] At the motel's pools, at least for a short time, the big men are able to disregard the judgments that society makes about different body types—who can intermingle with whom—and partake in sensuous spectacle. In her article "Taking the Waters," Wann states: "Water seeks its own level; and by a similar process of community, bodies are equal and unique in baths."[27] Likewise, the big men experience the healing sense of community that water, the great equalizer, provides.

Located in a gay enclave, in a gay motel, with everything from gay bars and restaurants to a gay gift shop all in the same compound, the Super Weekend at the Cabana comprises a gay ecological unit. This ecosystem can be viewed as a "total institution," as Goffman coined the term. By "total institution," Goffman refers to an asylum that is cut off from the rest of the world, where one undergoes resocialization.[28] Patrick Easto and Marcello Truzzi apply Goffman's concept to carnivals. They argue that, like a total institution, a carnival is a "highly integrated social and cultural system with strong boundaries maintained between itself and the community in which it is temporarily stationed. . . . [L]argely self-contained, [it] has its own distinctive culture, and maintains a separate social structure."[29] Indeed, the Super Weekend is a self-contained cultural system that offers temporary respite. By Easto and Truzzi's definition, it would be a sideshow of the "real" gay scene. And when viewed as institutionalized tourism, it would get a purely negative appraisal, seen as a compulsory "ghetto" big men must go to in order to belong, having run out of options. Nonetheless, as the big men themselves say, they are glad it exists, as it offers them a much-needed respite. Rather than be stripped of their fat identity as would happen at a total institution like a "fat camp," the men appreciate gaining recognition here for who they are. The insular, artificial environment of the Cabana provides them with a "realm of pure possibility,"[30] where they feel liberated at least for the duration of the weekend, seeking comfort in sheer numbers large enough for them to buy out a whole hotel.

In the carnivalesque atmosphere of the Cabana, the big men use campy humor to work through the stigma of being fat. Using camp, they poke fun at popular cultural forms by inverting them into their most bastardized renditions, thereby performing a "queer deconstruction of the opposition between 'original' and 'copy.'"[31] For example, one would think of synchronized swimming as a water dance performed by graceful, thin women in glamorous suits. When the big men at the Cabana mimic this dance, they turn it into a spectacle as they merrily slosh around. Through the lens of Sontag, the big men's campy water sport thus "proposes itself seriously, but cannot be taken altogether seriously because it is 'too much.'"[32]

By using sophisticated humor, the big men overcome their underdog status, albeit temporarily. Thus, Cleto's notion of camp as a survivalist strategy works through "a reinscription of stigma."[33] In Bateson's words, "this is play."[34] Bateson describes the edginess and seductive properties of play in his book *Steps to an Ecology of Mind*. He also describes play as being therapeutic, safely taking place on the playground. The Cabana, then, provides an enormous playground for grownups, where big men can socialize and explore their sexuality with impunity.

This weekend at the Cabana is a moral holiday for the big gay men. It is all about sexualizing. It gives couples a license to do as they please, because "what happens in Vegas stays in Vegas." Some couples arrive having already agreed to have an open relationship over the course of the Super Weekend. While there, they need not get permission from each other to mess around, and they can still be a couple when they return home. However, signals *can* get crossed, muddying their definition of "play." There may be a few couples who did not iron out the rules of engagement and may not be prepared for the enticing playful environment that makes it next to impossible to resist the come-ons. As a newcomer to the Super Weekend, I was told a cautionary tale about how things can go awry. The organizers told me that one year at the Cabana, a guy who saw his boyfriend having sex with someone else hurled a chair at them through the window in a fit of rage. Apparently, he was not aware of any agreement between them about opening up their relationship to outsiders. Indeed, play can get messy, as it has the potential to go too far.[35]

From Alienation to Rejuvenation

At the Cabana, the big men escape the world that stereotypes all fat people as slovenly, lazy, and unhealthy; in particular, they break from the gay community that renders them asexual and undesirable. For a few precious days, being "big" is not an issue, nor is being "gay." Yet, these markers *are* an issue for the big men who go there, because the gay community's rejection of them fuels their anxieties surrounding their wish to be recognized as being "sexual." Thus, the big men go to Girth & Mirth reunions to take back their power and to differentiate themselves as sexy, attractive, desirable, fun-loving, and human. Their acts of redifferentiation make fat something else; they change the singular, negative associations about fat that everyone knows and instead make being "big" special. In so doing, the big men become less self-conscious about their bodies.

The Girth & Mirth reunion brings together big men alienated in a world that renders them invisible because of their size, as it similarly renders older people invisible because of their age. Ironically, it is their weight and ample size that makes the big men both invisible and highly visible, at the same time. For example, a fat man may present the symptoms of a cold and be given a lecture about losing weight because in the doctor's eyes being fat overrides all of his other characteristics and symptoms. In fact, whenever the big men have the choice to let their size garner any benefits, they seem hesitant to claim disability status. Being well aware of this, the organizers of the Super Weekend chub-chaser contest purposefully omitted the "occupation" line from the entry form because they knew some guests who came to the weekend were on disability, and they did not want to embarrass them. So they were tiptoeing around the subject.

During the Super Weekend, big men have a chance to affirm the overriding characteristic of being fat by calling attention to other characteristics that equally define them. The Super Weekend carries the burden of creating hypervisibility. It provides an outlet whereby big men can show off the body excess. It is important to note that the big men seem to be less interested in normalizing their bodies than in expanding what qualifies as sexuality. Elsewhere, seeking sexual activity when one is fat and gay gets labeled as "sexual deviance," triply stigmatizing the big man. At their weekend reunion, playful sexualizing enables the big men to carve out a place for themselves at least in the margins of the gay community as fat and happy, though still not escaping the stereotype of jolly fat men.

Big men process shame in a number of ways, including internalizing it. As Goffman suggests in his sheltering discussion in *Stigma*, "whether we interact with strangers or intimates, we will find the fingertips of society have reached bluntly into the contact, even here putting us in our place."[36] Thus, at the big men's weekend retreat, although the shamers are not really there, in some sense, they are—and this shame gets played out in the big men's performances. So, a major response to shame appears to be play. Rather than use politics or lobbying,[37] the big men use the expressive culture of adult play at the Cabana to transvaluate their stigma. They engage in campy-queer behaviors, being funny and mirthful and having a laugh at their own expense. Through play, they dispute, refute, and rearrange meaning.

As a frame for the Super Weekend, play helps Girth & Mirthers renegotiate their value. For example, in the aquatic sports parody and the makeout session between the chasers, the big men turn on its head the criterion of the "ideal" body in determining dominance in the gay hierarchy, when the chubs are placed above the chasers and get to run the show. This reversal, as discussed earlier, is termed by Barbara Babcock "symbolic inversion." It "inverts, contradicts, abrogates, or in some fashion presents an alternative to commonly held cultural codes, values, and norms," creating the possibility of a "reversible world."[38] Babcock also calls it "institutionalized clowning"[39] that enables the performers to let off steam.

Through play, the big men trouble the codes of the gay hierarchy. Play communicates on different levels, conveying different messages. Babcock advocates: "We seem to need 'a margin of mess,' a category of 'inverted beings' both to define and to question the orders by which we live."[40] So, play can also be a way to interrogate the powers that be. One might imagine that some of the implicit messages of play, like the inverted gay hierarchy, would carry over into the big men's everyday lives. Play throws things off balance. It casts "the clean with the filthy, the rational with the animalistic, the ceremonial with the carnivalesque in order to maintain cultural vitality."[41] By troubling accepted behaviors, values, and norms, big men at the Cabana play with who they are, creating disorder as they shamelessly perform their fat bodies. Therefore, while these defiant acts of theirs may be shameful, they are, nonetheless, liberatory.

4

Big Gay Men's Struggle for Class Distinction

At the urging of a few members of the Ohio Girth & Mirth board, I made a point to also attend Convergence, which they thought would have a rather different atmosphere than that of the Super Weekend. Both events take place in a U.S. city annually—the former in July, the latter over Labor Day weekend. Unlike the joint effort of multiple groups that coordinate the Super Weekend, the group hosting Convergence changes every year, as does the location. Some of the same people attend both events, yet they sometimes dress and behave differently. Each event provides for big gay tourism in different ways, which begs a comparative analysis. At both, carnival offers the possibility for the mixing of classes and the abandoning of sexual mores.[1] The events differ from one another, however, in how they approach status differentiation: While the Super Weekend revels in the slum aspect of carnival, Convergence offers festival activities to elevate the big gay men's diminished status.

Compared with the Super Weekend, Convergence is a much larger event, with 500 to 1,000 guests.[2] When I attended in 2007, the numbers were down to 350, which was still twice the size of the Super Weekend. As Pyle and Loewy note, this fluctuation in recent numbers was due to folks' still feeling disgruntled over not receiving refunds when the New

Orleans event was canceled after Hurricane Katrina hit in 2005.[3] In any case, over Labor Day weekend, one brave club agrees to take charge of the event and have it on its home turf. The weekend has backing from the umbrella organization, Affiliated Bigmen's Clubs (ABC), formed to help advance awareness of big men's convergences within the gay community.

The context for each event differs. Unlike the motel for the Super Weekend, which is inexpensive and gay-exclusive, surrounded by a gay village, the Marriott in Minneapolis where Convergence is held this year is upscale and, though gay-friendly, is located in the midst of other mainstream events sharing some of the same spaces at the hotel as these men. Standing in stark contrast to the Cabana Inn with its closeted space and safe and familiar surroundings that provide an escape from hetero-normative society, the Minneapolis Marriott allows for cross-cultural encounters to take place between gay and straight guests. In fact, as I was taking the elevator up to my room Saturday before dinner, an elderly World War II veteran and his wife were talking with other fellow veterans in their military garb. They were all attending an event taking place at the hotel over the same weekend. Like a fly on the wall, I passed with my thin privilege. Unaware of my affiliation with the Girth & Mirthers, the veteran said to his wife and friends, "I'm dying to see what's on deck for those people who are all about 300 pounds." His remarks seemed to exoticize the big men, and his reference to them as "those people" brought home for me the "othering" big men suffer.

Convergence is foremost a group vacation and continues to rely on the presence of a gay social scene in large and diverse host cities to provide the itinerary for its excursions. Some include sightseeing more characteristic of mainstream tourism, supplemental to the more hotel-bound activities like those offered at the Super Weekend, such as cocktail receptions, pool parties, buffet meals, and the Chub-and-Chaser Contest. Convergence also offers educational seminars and a theme dance. A variety of rather elaborate packages list the à la carte prices, such as $30 for attending the Renaissance Festival or $20 to go to the casino. These expenditures are above and beyond the cost of the hotel and registration for the event. Many of the guests also tack onto their packages a Convergence t-shirt, which begins at size LG and goes up to 6XL, immediately excluding all of the slim chasers in this inverted world.

Convergence is a more pricey vacation than the Super Weekend at the Cabana, and one more aligned with the host city's already existing mainstream tourism, thus making the guests purveyors of culture. Here, the men engage in status-affirming activities. When the guests go on city tours and outings to gay bars, the mall, the state fair, the sculpture garden, or the art center together, or when they attend events in the hotel like the autumn-themed buffet and dance, they engage in some of the legitimate activities they feel they missed out on in their lives, such as tailgate parties or their high school prom. The normalizing activities at Convergence, such as sightseeing or the theme dance, are some of the ways the big gay men assimilate toward middle-class heterosexual society. The gay big men's ways of performing class create an extra obligation on the event—that is, to perform class is value-added, not just recompense like at the Super Weekend. To seek status, they have to silence the discourses of shame that undermine their class-based efforts to distinguish themselves through "Culture at Convergence" (fittingly, the title of a meeting-packet insert the year I attended).[4]

Unlike those who attend the Super Weekend, Labor Day weekenders still perform some of the markers of the mainstream middle class. In so doing, the gay big men experience themselves as less "deviant," less on the fringes of society. For Convergence-goers, cultural outings contribute to the "social betterment" of the guests, signaling middle-class aspirations. The Convergence tactic, in a Bourdieuian sense, is one of "up-classing" or "up-class" distinction: the illusion that if members of a disenfranchised group mimic the elite, doing so will raise their own status. This behavior corresponds to Bourdieu's model well and conforms to stereotypes about gay men generally.[5] It hurts those who feel they do not live up to the stereotype that all gay men are stylish dressers or have perfect bodies. These weekend events poke fun at this stereotype, while at the same time toying with the positive stereotype of all gay men being aesthetically inclined to good tastes, although it is reductive and inaccurate to believe this.

When I first began to consider attending Convergence, the super-chub with whom I later traveled to the event offered some comparisons of it to the Super Weekend at the Cabana. His impression of the Super Weekend was that it is "more 'play'-oriented, whereas Convergence runs the gamut with fashion shows, big fashion designers creating leatherwear made to order for all shapes and sizes, body image workshops, formal dinners, and 'nicer' accommodations, by far." Space is also reserved in the hotel for the gay vendor market and movie showings. On our drive to the event, my travel companion, who had attended several Convergences, reminisced one year that the headliner was a disabled comedian; then they had a masquerade night for which the guests were given fancy feather masks to wear; another year, there was a French jazz singer; and another time, the hired entertainment was drag. All of these events cost money—and anytime a group has hired entertainment, it is safe to assume that members of the group have disposable income. In contrast, the Super Weekenders choose to meet at a cheap motel that advertises monthly rates.

At Convergence, the big men preferred to differentiate their status from that of other fat men by wearing sharp and classy attire. For instance, as my travel companion also recalled, at a past Convergence, Casual Male, a mainstream clothing chain, sponsored a fashion runway show catering to the needs of men who wore sizes XL and up, and outfitted pairs of chubs and chasers who walked down the runway together. The guests could then buy these outfits at 50 percent off. During the Super Weekend, differentiating oneself through fashion meant wearing playwear like leather chaps and body harnesses. Then there were some big men who wore handmade caftans or tie-dyed tees that a Girth & Mirther sold out of a makeshift shop in one of the motel rooms.

The choice of attire at both Convergence and the Super Weekend reflects the different approaches the big men take to representing their alienated bodies, which also says something about their struggle with class distinction.[6] At Convergence, there appears to be an interest in style, as was illustrated in the fashion show sponsored by Casual Male. In contrast at the Super Weekend, the oversized tie-dyed tees and handmade caftans for sale simply represent functional apparel. Tie-dyeing is a cheap, accessible way to create customized clothing with its psychedelic, countercultural origin. Bourdieu analyzes differing approaches to clothing the body as follows.

> The doubly prudent choice of the garment that is both "simple" ("versatile," "all-purpose"), i.e., as little marked and as unrisky as possible ("no-nonsense," "practical"), and [a] "good value for [the] money," i.e., cheap and long-lasting, no doubt presents itself as the most reasonable strategy, given . . . the economic and cultural capital (not to mention time) that can be invested in buying clothes.[7]

Bourdieu distinguishes between investing in body comfort and putting the body at ease and investing in clothing to garner cultural capital or living a stylized life that displays one's economic freedom and status.[8] Indeed, some Super Weekenders enjoy their light-as-air, generously sized caftans, borrowed from the repertoire of plus-sized women's clothing but resignified as pool leisure wear, as they stroll from their bedrooms to the poolside for cocktails. On the other hand, sending down the runway men modeling mainstream designer brands for big men, such as Calvin Klein, Dockers, Kenneth Cole, Tommy Hilfiger, and Nautica, signals the guests' desire for greater distinction.

First-Timers' Orientation

First-time guests got introduced to the two settings quite differently. Whereas during the Super Weekend it appeared that hazing was the way to learn the sexual codes of the weekend, at Convergence there was an actual First-Timers' Orientation. This was held, as most orientations are, at 8:00 in the morning on the second day. By then, folks had already had a taste of Convergence culture. The new president of ABC facilitated the orientation. At the Super Weekend, I was one of the organizers; but at the Labor Day weekend, I was simply one of the new guests. Eight of us newcomers attended the orientation and sat in a small talking circle in one of the hotel's meeting rooms. The following is an excerpt from my fieldnotes of that morning.

> While we were waiting to begin, the facilitator mentioned he hoped one newbie in particular would show up. He said the man felt a bit overwhelmed at his first night of Convergence because he comes from a small town and wasn't used to an all-gay environment where guys were kissing, holding hands, and hugging. He added this is why the orientation was on the second day after the guests had some experience with the event and were looking for a debriefing. He also told us he wasn't a trained counselor, saw no need to talk in clinical terms, and we should all feel free to use sexual slang and refer frankly to genitalia.

The facilitator's pseudo-professional lingo reminded me again of the mainstream traits of Convergence, which were so unlike those of the Super Weekend. The timing of the orientation session, which was following one night of exposure to the sexual undercurrent at Convergence, also pointed to the tendency toward a formal organization, wherein members are first exposed to and later debriefed on what they just experienced.

The Convergence orientation was reminiscent of a sex-ed class, where the participants were encouraged to talk openly with the trusted facilitator about any burning questions they might have. And people did have questions, though some were off topic. The facilitator gave them advice about sexual expectations and on how to deal with advances from the other guests. The sexual scene Convergence promised was in sharp contrast with what my compatriots had told me to expect from the Super Weekend. As the Convergence facilitator told us during orientation, "If you come to Convergence just for sex, you may leave disappointed. If you come to meet a lot of good people and make new friends, and then if the sex happens, that's a bonus." The advice I had heard from my informants at the Cabana about the Super Weekend was different: "If you come to the Super Weekend looking for a long-term relationship to blossom from casual sexual encounters, you'll be sorely disappointed."

The facilitator at Convergence also gave a tip on how to reject people and reminded folks to retain their personal values. As he put it, "If you're not interested in someone, gently tell him, 'You're not my type' and if he gets nasty, he probably was not the kind of person you would want to be with, anyway." At the Super Weekend, it seemed this advice would not fly— why else would one be there? In fact, the answer that worked at the Cabana, which I had to learn by trial and error, was "I don't play." Relationship advice given at Convergence was packaged in a formal presentation. Furthermore, the recommendation given for how to deal with unwanted attention was unusually mainstream. Participants were advised to assert an individual standard for why they might respond negatively to someone's advances. In contrast, at the Super Weekend, I had to crack the cultural codes of sex play.

The Convergence facilitator contrasted the Labor Day weekend with Bear runs where people are more overtly sexual and rowdy in public spaces, whereas at Convergence folks may be a bit more reserved. As he said, "Here, guests meet at the pool and take it back to their room, though occasionally you'll see things during the wee hours of the morning in the hospitality suite." Then he opened the floor to any questions or concerns folks might have, asking whether anyone felt uncomfortable. One guy chimed in saying, "I just went to Fire Island, and this was nothing in comparison." Indeed, there was less sex on display at Convergence than at the Super Weekend. Sex took place behind closed doors—again hearkening to middle-class mainstream etiquette and rules regarding PDA—not that this event too did not include plenty of fondling in the pool.

My Researcher/Participant Status

Being more overtly a researcher at Convergence put me in a different position from the one I was in at the Super Weekend. My travel companion, trained in social work, advised me to talk openly about my role as a researcher and suggested saying I was writing about how big gay men work through self-esteem issues. He felt that with this approach, more people would talk to me. Taking his advice, I introduced myself and my study to the weekend guests whenever I was able to engage in a longer conversation with someone. However, being a participant observer did not exempt me from getting drawn into full participation. In fact, during the Chub-and-Chaser Contest, I found myself being dragged onto the stage.

While I was still enjoying the luxury of being a researcher on the sidelines, I mentally noted some differences between the contest at Convergence and the version at the Super Weekend. The former was streamlined, without all of the traditional beauty pageant categories in which the contestants at the Super Weekend competed and mocked, such as the question-and-answer section, individual talent performances, and the group dance. The Convergence contest was simpler. It consisted of individualized dance routines that were more carefully thought out and less off-the-cuff. Also, it was judged more traditionally, with a panel of three judges, whereas at the Super Weekend the entire audience was the judge, giving power to the people, so to speak.

The line between the performers and spectators at Convergence was easy to cross: The performers were not separated from the spectators by a platform stage and railings as at the Super Weekend. The stage at Convergence was distinguishable only by who was performing on the parquet floor and who was sitting at tables on the carpeted end of the same ballroom. Therefore, before I knew it, I was literally being pulled out of my seat at the dinner table and onto the stage by a chub contestant as one of his two chaser sidekicks. The following excerpt is from my fieldnotes reconstructed after the Chub Contest:

A chub from the U.K. came out in a light button-up shirt and black pants. I later learned he worked in politics and his boyfriend was from Sweden. He walked out cracking his leather belt. Knowing what was coming, I shifted nervously in my seat—like at a comedy club or drag show, when you're sitting up front, and it's inevitable you're going to be pulled into the routine. He came toward our table, beckoning me. He wrapped his belt around me and pulled me from the table to the stage.

While we were on stage and the music was playing, he gently whispered some quick instructions to me. I obliged with my best improv, for which my dinner companions later complimented me. I had to get on my knees and undo Mr. U.K.'s shirt, then take off mine. He pulled out baby oil, and we oiled each other up. Then he spanked me on the behind with his belt. He also pulled in one of the Asian chasers and like at a carwash, we both oiled his chest on either side.

When I returned to my seat, my dinner companions threw me their napkins so I could wipe myself off. My travel companion then wiped my back and showed me the photographs he took.

As I discovered through this unexpected turn of events, even though I was more or less out as a researcher, there was no way I was going to be able to sit back and simply watch the show. This full-blown participation had been required of me at the Super Weekend, as well. But there, it was to be expected, because I had not spoken openly about my research.

Dorothy Noyes has remarked on the problem of an onlooker in a festival setting, who inevitably gets swept up into the crowd.[9] Indeed, during my time at various Girth & Mirth events, I experienced a kind of recruitment taking place, as people assumed I must be a chaser—why else would I be interested in the lives of chubs? I did not, in so many words, try to contradict the assumptions projected onto me. Rather, I accepted the roles in which they placed me.

Chaser Cachet

Most important to the focus of this chapter, there was more chaser action at Convergence where, through the lens of status, big gay men appeared to value anyone who would give them greater validation. Altogether, there

were fewer contestants at Convergence, where the chasers took their performances rather seriously. They made their appearance on stage in the
reverse order from the way they did at the Super Weekend, where chubs
tend to be a valued commodity or affirmed group and therefore are saved
for last. So at Convergence, the chubs went first, five followed by six chasers;
at the Super Weekend, the chasers went first, six followed by nine chubs.

As soon as the chub part of the contest was completed, the gay big
men in the audience rushed the stage, getting in position to take photographs of the chasers who were about to take center stage, something
that did not happen during the chub portion of the contest. They wanted
to record these hypervisual sex objects, each with its own beguiling persona, each employing a stereotype of the prototypical male. My fieldnotes
from that evening read as follows:

> Among the chasers, there was a brawny, tanned guy, all oiled up, wearing
> only a loincloth and on his head a crown of ivy. Another chaser, an African
> American, came out in football garb, dancing to the lyrics, "don'tcha wish
> your girlfriend was hot like me?" A third, who I learned was a disciplinary
> principal at a Chicago Catholic school, bounced onto the stage with a drill,
> his elastic underwear band for a toolbelt, dancing to "Macho Man." Yet
> another chaser was a German man, wearing a leather harness and thong,
> cracking a cat-o'-nine-tails. Then there was Devanté, who danced to the
> lyrics "loosen up my buttons" in his white bikini briefs. I recognized him
> from the Super Weekend at the Cabana, where he had stolen the contest
> earlier this summer. Finally, there was the "twink," with a retro-eighties
> look. He wore a leather thong and sensually moved to a dance remake of
> McKenzie's "San Francisco."

These chasers at Convergence were all clearly 100 percent chaser mate-
rial, unlike those at the Super Weekend, many of whom were in fact
big guys who liked chasing big guys. Devanté won the chaser contest at
Convergence as he had done at the Super Weekend—perhaps working
his way up to becoming the doll of the chub-chaser circuit.

Chasers appear to carry greater cachet at Convergence, while chubs are more desirable at the Super Weekend. This difference may be because Convergence is more of a chub-chaser event, while the ethos at the Super Weekend is more big men–for–big men. At Convergence, big gay men, who are increasingly relegated to a low status, have a chance to flirt and romantically associate with their "trophy chasers," thereby elevating their status by proxy, albeit temporarily.

Given my research goal to give voice to big gay men, I spoke more to chubs at Convergence than to chasers. This misstep is reflected in the fact that the information I have on chasers is secondhand. Interviewing chasers to learn more about them would have enabled me to appreciate their subject position, which big men consider to be a difficult one to maintain within most gay circles.

The super-chub who was gracious enough to share his transportation and lodgings with me served as my gatekeeper at Convergence. He introduced me to several key figures, most of whom were big gay men. It was he who first made me aware of the difficult position in which chasers find themselves. As he said, "Chasers feel stigma because they pursue gay 'misfits.'" I take this to mean "courtesy stigma" in the way Goffman coined the term. Goffman observes that people who associate with a stigmatized group are guilty by association, so to speak, as they are conferred a courtesy stigma.[10] In her discussion of male heterosexual fat admirers, Millman also hints at the same phenomenon.[11] This came up in a conversation I had with a Girth & Mirth member who was working as a vendor at Convergence, selling CDs of his stand-up comedy and dance music compilations. He told me chasers usually experience a stigma by association. He continued:

This is the one time a year they can come and be comfortable expressing their desires. There is this chaser who settled down with a conventionally handsome guy because he is so closeted about his sexual preferences. And he wanted to be "normal"—like homosexual guys who marry women. But he has to sneak off to Convergence once a year to get his groove on.

It is noteworthy that chasers, like chubs, worry about their status, but for a different reason: Their reputations can be tarnished if they are seen going out with men of larger stature. Chasers who associate with chubs may be marginally accepted within this socially "deviant" group as honorary members. However, if they were to come out as "chasers" among gay "normals," they would likely be tainted for holding an unorthodox ideal of what constitutes an "appropriate" mate.

Chub/Chaser Dynamics

In both heterosexual and gay society, there are chub/chaser subcultures. In the heterosexual main, men of a larger stature are still desirable to some women, without being relegated to the margins of society because of their fat bodies. But in the gay main, it would be rare for a big man to be desirable to other gay men, his bulk forcing him to seek sexual validation on the fringes. It is in response to big gay men's abject corporeal status that Girth & Mirth organizes events such as those at Convergence and the Super Weekend.

It is ironic that chasers should be called "chasers" at all, because they are not exactly chasing, but being chased. A couple of different chubs at Convergence lamented about chasers' being intentionally ambiguous, playing hard to get. One of the big men remarked over dinner: "I would prefer if a chaser just said 'yes' or 'no'; but instead, they act politely uninterested. They're just so damn indirect." The principle of least interest appears to be in operation here. Perhaps Madonna says it best in her song "Justify My Love": "Poor is the man whose pleasures depend on the permission of another."[12] The ratio of chasers to chubs in the United States is off; chasers are in low supply, therefore in high demand. So, they can be noncommittal, stringing along several big men even over one short weekend. In contrast, chubs are a dime a dozen, constituting a generic pool from which chasers pick and choose. Within Convergence culture, chasers have more power that comes with their status as a rare commodity, such that they can afford to be teases.

Admittedly, within the chub/chaser dynamic there is potential to expand the "acceptable" range of body types any gay man may choose in his sex partner. However, not all of the chasers' sexual pursuits of big men should be lauded as being counterhegemonic. The big man who gave me a ride to Convergence told me that as a super-chub who loves to meet up with chasers, he knows of "some chasers at Convergence who get into packs and plan their conquests—they are the bed-notchers. They huddle together deciding on the biggest guy and who can use him in bed. Then they keep score of their conquests and compare notes. Not all chasers do this, but some do." If this big man's opinion is representative of those of the Girth & Mirthers, then chasers are sometimes regarded as being predatorial.

In his chapter on teams, Goffman refers to this as "dramaturgical cooperation."[13] That is, these chasers act as co-conspirators who cooperate to stage a performance of sexual conquest. While this may not constitute the "hogging" that some heterosexual men do to fat women, as discussed by Ariane Prohaska and Jeannine Gailey, it indeed makes sex a sport.[14] For instance, Carol Gardner talks of public harassment that men in teams dole out to women, "scoring" them based on appearance as though it were all fun and games.[15] This interpretation of sexual conquest as bed-notching and as something to be frowned upon was not the case at the Super Weekend, where a chub won the Doorknob Award for having scored the highest number of sexual encounters. Furthermore, at the Super Weekend, it was a chub, not a chaser, who was the sexual conquistador.

These power differentials do not necessarily mean that chubs and chasers never commit to each other in a long-term relationship. Yet there seems to be a built-in instability. In one case at Convergence, a middle-aged chub told me that he has been in a relationship with a younger chaser for the past four years. In fact, they were at Convergence celebrating their anniversary together, only having recently moved to the host city. The chub was the director of a human services agency, where he hired his boyfriend as a secretary. As he told me,

The current problem is that my intellectual needs are going unmet. I feel like I'm being forced into a fathering role. Then again, my partner's sexual needs are not being met completely, either: he likes to play around. One time, I was intimidated by his playing with a guy I thought was better-looking than me. Then this other time, he got mad at me because I was talking to a guy for several hours. He sobbed later in the evening about it.

We all witnessed this chub, who had refrained from alcohol for a year, go on a drinking binge during this particular weekend at Convergence. On the second night there, we also witnessed that, while he looked out over the pool from his bedroom window, he could see his chaser behaving like a bad boy, pleasuring other men under water. This display resembled the sexual dynamic of the fat mother and the thin, provocative child mentioned in Millman's work.[16] In this case, it is one of a chub daddy and his dependent chaser son. The downside to all of this is that the chub has to be a nurturer and tolerate his chaser's naughty and disrespectful behavior, or be a disciplinarian to a misbehaving man-child—either way, what used to be an enjoyable, sexy roleplay begins to get a little old after a while.

Replacement Culture

As in all love and communication, there can be tender moments, not just disappointing heartbreaks; and Convergence provides opportunities for big gay men to have some semblance of romance they might otherwise have missed out on. It gives them a chance to engage in replacement activities to make up for lost time. The year I attended, the Chub-and-Chaser Contest at Convergence was followed by the Fall Harvest Dance Party, which was the big gay men's version of a homecoming dance. This was a departure from the Super Weekend itinerary, wherein folks came out of the contest and moved on to sexualizing in the pool. The only dancing on the agenda at the Super Weekend was during the contest, when men horsed around shirtless, mocking anything that would come remotely close to a formal dance.

The Fall Harvest Dance Party at Convergence had a traditional flavor, one that made it look familiar to me. It was not a mockery, nor was it reminiscent of a gay circuit party, a subcultural club scene popularized in the 1980s and '90s. It could have easily been imported from mainstream high school culture. With the lights dimmed down low, big men danced to popular Top 40 music in the ballroom, while others sat at candle-lit tables with white linen tablecloths, talking quietly. Some walked up to the DJ to request a favorite song. The dance offered another occasion that afforded a mixing of classes, with chubs and chasers intermingling. As I learned from my travel companion, in a different year at Convergence, it was a joy to hear a song with multivalent meaning, as was the case when the gay big men got down on the dance floor, singing and boogieing to k.d. lang's "Big-Boned Gal."[17] Multivalent recognition requires what Bourdieu refers to as "cultural competency," which is a set of knowledge structures needed to stretch whom the song-maker had in mind as the intended audience for this song in order to include not only the proud and entranc-ing, "a-rockin'" and a-dancin' big-boned gals, but also big-boned guys.[18] Along the same lines, the Super Weekenders' reinterpretation of everyday objects, such as reimagining a crystal doorknob as a trophy, also demon-strates a level of cultural competency. As Bourdieu observes, being able to aestheticize even the most banal of objects shows cultural sophistication.[19]

On the whole, the dance at Convergence had many recognizable mainstream features, such as a slow dance and a cash bar. One might imagine that events like this offer big gay men compensation for perhaps missing out on prom night or their homecoming dance in high school. The event signaled toward mainstream culture and provided a belated occasion that gay big men, who might have been unable to go to a prom because they did not meet mainstream standards for size and/or sexual-ity, could attend this dance instead, even if years later. In this fashion, Convergence enables big gay men to take part in replacement activities and do what all other people get to do, gay or straight.

Other minority groups also have replacement traditions. For exam-ple, there are immigrant dances that blur the line between American traditions and those of other cultures. American Muslims have girls-only proms. Or Latinos living in the United States co-opt American cultural markers into Quinceañera, their coming-of-age Latina prom. In these subcultures, as in the case of the Girth & Mirth subculture, there is a paradox. While seemingly striving for traditional activities, members of these groups seem to be saying, "We are *not* mainstream, but we're going to '*do* mainstream' our way."[20]

The Question of Class at Convergence

Convergence is perceived to be classier than the Super Weekend all the way around, and guests are funneling more money into it. Big men who opt out of Convergence in favor of the Super Weekend regard the former as a high-class event. One Girth & Mirther who never goes to Convergence because of the cost said, "Convergence is out of most people's budgets, whereas the Super Weekend makes for an affordable run, and Bear Camp is an affordable run, too." According to folklore circulating among the tried-and-true Super Weekenders, on the first night of Convergence people dress up; they even wear suits and ties. However, the year I attended, I learned that while guests do look nice for dinner, it is certainly not a black-tie event. Yet, relatively speaking, Convergence-goers appear more conservative to the Super Weekenders. Bourdieu describes such conservatism as the appeal of trying to look presentable or better than one's peers, in order to measure up to conservative values.[21] For stigmatized groups, such as big gay men, performances of tastefulness are sometimes used to counter abjection.

As an outsider to Convergence culture, the same Girth & Mirther above speculated on the connection between money and masculinity. He suggested that the higher a man's social class, the lower his masculinity. He regarded Labor Day weekenders as rich old queens. He said, "They stay at high-class hotels. How can I put it? I would expect you would see the queeny side of everybody at Convergence." Hearing this statement reinforced for me that the Girth & Mirthers share the same anxiety as the big, hirsute Bears regarding their masculinity. I saw that in his anxiety to hold on to his own masculine status in a relational world, the speaker above chose to distance himself from what he perceived as the "big ol' queens" at Convergence.[22]

Many of the activities at Convergence approach those one would expect to find at a traditional conference. The social environment at the Labor Day weekend affords the possibility for networking and pursuing shared interests in addition to sexualizing. For instance, the Convergence I attended had a seminar on fat fetishism. Sitting in a hotel conference room, those of us who attended the seminar became students together who were all critical consumers of the information we were receiving. During the presentation, an older big man challenged the speaker on the topic of intentionally gaining weight with the pressure of an encouraging partner.[23] When he said he was a member of the National Association to Advance Fat Acceptance, I thought he might share my interest in critical fat studies. Recognizing him as a fellow academic, I was able to bring up my own professional identity when the session broke up and we talked. I eventually learned he was a professor of psychology.[24] It was surprising to me to have a forum that sparked our ability to assert our occupational identities and educational status and talk shop. It is harder to imagine this kind of mutual intellectual recognition happening at an everyman's event like the Super Weekend.

Similar occasions at Convergence afforded the possibility for the guests to perform their identities very differently from what guests were able to do at the Super Weekend. However, my ability to engage in an academic exchange with the psychology professor was perhaps more a function of my having been encouraged to overtly acknowledge my researcher status at Convergence. I was able to share my identity as a gay scholar, in part because of the social class of the clientele at Convergence who can accept and even be flattered by a researcher's validation. At the Super Weekend, in contrast, my travel companions thought it would be better if I kept my researcher status under wraps.

Convergence's class consciousness became apparent when I compared the way raffle ticket sales were handled at Convergence with the way they were handled at Super Weekend. At Convergence, with the event being so large, tickets were simply sold, with little thought given to creative selling techniques. At the Super Weekend, organizers took a different approach: Tickets were wrapped around the buyer's waist, his girth determining the number of tickets he would get for the set price—the greater his girth, the more he was worth. The Super Weekend tradition has been to use raffle ticket sales as an opportunity to flip the script on privileging petite waistlines, thereby engaging in creative activism. It is not surprising, though, that no matter how innovative the Super Weekenders were, Convergence's raffle brought in a bigger kitty than did the Super Weekend's—$1,200 versus $890—given the greater number of guests at Convergence. The class-conscious streak of guests at Convergence also came to the fore when raffle prizes were handed out. Among the prizes was a free night stay at Motel 6. But the winners acted reluctant to claim the prize, as though this low-end motel were beneath them. This would be unheard of at the Super Weekend, because the event itself is literally held in the equivalent of a gay Motel 6.

One of the markers of the U.S. Convergence is its international representation, signaling cosmopolitanism, which is less explicitly about hierarchy and more about another kind of cultural capital: U.S. multicultural capital.[25] For example, the Convergence I attended had guests from Sweden, Germany, and the U.K., and many from Asian countries. In fact, there is also a European big men's Convergence, the counterpart to the U.S. Convergence. In the case of the Asian chasers, it appeared they were drawn into the scene by the greater ratio of big men in the United States. Then there was even a contest to see who had traveled the farthest distance to Convergence. The year I attended, the winner was a Japanese man who had come halfway across the globe.

Finally, the two events, Convergence and the Super Weekend, are indicators of *how* gay big men socially construct their culture differently. Convergence maintains a more mainstream profile, whereas the Super Weekend creates a total institution, or a world set apart. In the former, the big men invoke class to move beyond the walls of the gay world by sightseeing or taking excursions to the art museum. In the latter, they are immersed for a weekend, among only their peers. This is not to say that the Super Weekend reunion is devoid of class performances. Instead, Super Weekenders invert the imposition of taste by poking fun at class markers, while Convergence-goers engage in "conspicuous consumption."[26]

Bourdieu suggests that cultural activities aimed at the taste of the masses elicit a greater degree of spectator involvement than those activities directed more toward bourgeois tastes.[27] Popular culture has a role at both big men's events, but the Super Weekend seeks to engage the defiant culture that belongs to Girth & Mirthers. Spectacle, laughter, and inversion abound at both events, but Convergence is more likely to also include things that occur at an aesthetic distance, like viewing sculpture or artwork during a cultural excursion.

Class at Convergence provides big gay men a resource to take part in the markers of middle-class society, such as proms and fashion shows. It is also a formal venue for middle-class gay big men to have an opportunity to sexualize. This class distinction between the two settings fundamentally changes how they perform their identities—at Convergence, through status differentiation and cultural activities; at the Super Weekend, through play and slummin' it.

5

Shame Reconfigured

Members of Girth & Mirth reconfigure their shame of being fat by performing their bodies as objects of desire. Yet becoming objects of desire and feeling sexy does not necessarily have to culminate in sex. Big men simply engage in defiant, in-your-face behaviors in an attempt to construct meaningful lives and carve out a place for themselves within the gay community. At times, they also attempt to effect real structural change by challenging gay body politics and the imposition of derogatory labels.

In this chapter, I focus on alternatives for reconfiguring shame other than the sexual objectification described in chapter 3 and the status-seeking described in chapter 4. Many go to their local Girth & Mirth club just to weather the stigma surrounding being a big man in the gay community. Girth & Mirthers in the local club I studied also work to transform fat shame by employing a variety of other reconfigurations. Among them is confronting their shamers, achieving group recognition through the Pride parade, campaigning for consumer inclusion, setting themselves apart by redefining what it means to be big and gay, or, as reflected in the club's mission, redefining their sullied identity as something positive, desirable, and joyous. Such joyful disregard of shame is aptly reflected in the name the big men have given their club: Girth & Mirth.

A Second Coming Out

To varying degrees and often at separate times, most Girth & Mirthers have come out as both gay and fat. As gay men, they are familiar with the "coming out" metaphor and can readily extend it to size acceptance. One big gay man shared: "I had a second coming out later in life, after my marriage ended. I think you come out twice: once to realize you're gay, and then to accept yourself as who you are; and if that's big, if that's being a big person, then so be it." As this big man moved away from his heterosexual orientation as a formerly married man, he felt more compelled to atone for his size because of the body consciousness imposed by gay culture. By his coming out as gay, any body image issues he might formally have had got intensified.

In the following story, another member told me about his big gay debut, sending in photospreads of his ample body in the nude for a gay magazine to help him break out of his body shyness:

> I gave a unique coming-out present to myself. Back in '96, I had lost around 70 to 80 pounds. I probably weighed about 240. So to me, I was actually in really good shape, but I still had the issue that I was shy about my body. A friend of mine in San Francisco had a big-men's magazine, so they asked my roommate and me to do a photospread. We had pictures taken and sent them in, and they said they were good, but could we do some more. As a joke, we put in a couple of pictures with watersports in them.[1] Well, they published them! It was like a good coming out present to myself. You don't see a whole lot of men my size in magazines.

With the support of his roommate, this big gay man confronted head-on being ashamed of his body. Though he had lost a significant amount of weight, seventy to eighty pounds by his own admission, this big man was still not over his body consciousness. It took his coming out as fat in a publication for big men to achieve a sense of self-acceptance. As he pointed out, he thus contributed to big men's visibility.

Acknowledging their girth, the big men find solidarity in a fatphobic world. As Michael Moon and Eve Sedgwick suggest, coming out and living openly as a fat and gay person involves taking a risk and stating the obvious: that one has a fat body.[2] That is, coming out as fat and gay involves owning one's size and sexuality. It lays claim to "a renegotiation of the *representational contract* between one's body and one's world."[3] The past president of the local Girth & Mirth club clearly articulates this size-positive group's campy-queer subtext: "We all love to see each other and spend quality time eating, laughing, being out, loud, proud, politically incorrect, big, and maybe, just maybe, a few blocks up Wrong Street. Okay, maybe a few miles up Wrong Street—and down a few alleys!" Indeed, it sometimes takes politically *incorrect* humor or going against the grain for gay big men to put themselves out there in the world.

As with other forms of everyday shame, big gay men engage in fat revolution together in monumental ways, converting their shame to pride publicly as they do every year during the Pride parade. But more often than not, this transformation happens through mundane aspects of everyday life like having dinners out or grabbing a cup of coffee together. As Britt and Heise so aptly put it, while "shame may lead to hiding, . . . pride may lead to expansive behaviors in public space."[4] Big men's growing sense of pride figuratively parallels their large body size, as reflected in language when one might say, "He swelled with pride."[5] When one is proud, one indeed feels bigger, taller, and stronger, and the protection and backing of one's fellow sufferers at Girth & Mirth appear to do a lot in terms of moving them in the direction of weathering their shame.

Weathering Shame

Shame's mercurial nature leaves people unsatisfied, which can actually be productive, leading them to take action. Those shamed may make a "commitment to more generous identities, responsibilities, and connections."[6] That is to say, some abject people are able to own up to and reconfigure the shame of being fat. As Sedgwick puts it, "[A]t least for certain ('queer') people, shame is simply the first, and remains a permanent, structuring fact of identity: one that . . . has its own, powerfully productive and powerfully social metamorphic possibilities."[7] The shame that big gay men feel for being fat fosters a sense of we-ness among those who choose to join the club—hence, how Girth & Mirth originally came about. By connecting with fellow stigmatized sufferers, big gay men are able to redress their shame.

Another form of reconfiguring shame is striking right back at the shamers. In some of the narratives about coping with being humiliated, Girth & Mirthers share how they reverse the roles by going on the offense and calling things on the carpet, rather than being on the defense. For instance, one big man said he felt strongly that it is important to challenge the verbal abuse meted out by those who bully him in public about his pronounced size. He said he believes in having it out with the shamer by coming back with a zinger that acknowledges the insult. As he put it, "I throw it right back at 'em, just to embarrass them back. I am all about public humiliation and embarrassment. If someone upsets me, if they say something about my size in public, even if it's innuendoes to suggest certain things, I will embarrass them. I strongly believe, call it on the carpet." This Girth & Mirther said he operates on the premise that if the bully "can't deal with it, then his own immature behavior gets exposed." He believes "everyone needs to know the shamer's maturity level and see the type of person he is and see what he would really be like behind the scenes." This modus operandi may not be the most constructive way to transform shame, because it only deflects it and reduces the victim to the level of perpetrator. For some, however, challenging routine harassment may be a possible strategy for dealing with shame.

Big men also feel targeted by medical professionals, whom they should be able to trust. Doctors themselves will even 'fess up to being sizist. As an ER doctor told one big man flat out, "When a big, middle-aged guy walks into the emergency room, that's going to be the first thing on every health professional's mind: this is a heart attack. That's just how it's going to be." Given the prejudicial treatment they encounter, Girth & Mirthers have taken to providing doctor referrals for one another. One big man who was dissatisfied with previous doctors who routinely profiled him eventually procured through trial and error a gay physician who was a big man himself. As he told me, "I found a fat doctor [chuckles]. He's also gay [chuckles again]." This big man went on to tell me that the new doctor he found complimented his good health and exercise habits. This assessment presents the possibility that health can be relative at any size. As the doctor reportedly told him,

> What other doctors don't know is that somebody like you, and somebody else as big as you walking down the street, you are infinitely healthier than that person. Because you watch your blood sugar, you take your blood pressure medicine, and you do everything you're supposed to do to be as healthy as you possibly can be. Yes, you're a big guy, but you are extremely healthy for a big guy.

This doctor, as recounted by this narrator, at least acknowledged that a big man can be healthy despite his size. However, his remark suggests there are "good" and "bad" fat patients. It also sets up another shame dichotomy of there being "healthy" versus "unhealthy" fat people.

Big men also manage their shame of being fat by attending occasions where they can find comfort in numbers. For instance, Girth & Mirthers rendezvous with members of other nearby big men's clubs on Pride Night at Kings Island amusement park in Mason, Ohio. This affords them the luxury of knowing that they are not the only big guys there. One Girth & Mirth member recalled the last time he went to Pride Night:

> At least we're able to go to a place like that, be open with each other, walk around holding hands, and still be able to ride some of the rides and have pizza and cotton candy and enjoy everything there is about an amusement

park as a gay couple. My partner and I have gone to it in years past, and we meet up with larger guys from all over town and the rest of Ohio, plus Indiana, West Virginia, Kentucky—and it's fun.

This speaker added that regionally, and luckily, there are a lot of big gay men where he is from, who organize groups of big men to attend Pride Night so that they are not in the minority. As he told me, "Maybe it's a midwestern thing, I don't know. I know that this other group in central Ohio also goes. And I know that our group tries to have some type of loosely organized thing to go to it, as well; so there's lots of us there." This big man also remarked that if they have to forgo a ride because of their waist size or weight, they are able to cope with their discomfort by using humor in the safety of one another's company. The more important point, however, is that gay big men are happier to be dealing with the issue of accessibility to rides that all fat people face, rather than not being able to enjoy Pride Night. At larger amusement parks like Disney World, Gay Days are less within big men's reach, because they are way outnumbered by those who meet the prevailing gay image norm.[8]

Improving Body Comfort

Girth & Mirth offers its members a valuable network. It also tries to reach out to other big gay men beyond the walls of the club. At their activities, Girth & Mirthers try to raise members' and visitors' self-confidence and body comfort. One gay big man complimented the club for its role in making members feel included and attractive, thus helping them recon-figure their sexual injury.

A key strength of Girth & Mirthers is they can make others feel comfort-able. Actually, sometimes I feel really sexy with them, because they tease me all the time about being a top. They say, "But you're a top, dammit!" And some of them think I'm good-looking. That's nice too, when they say you're good-looking; it's not that they want to get into your pants, they're just drawing you out. At Gay Pride, too, there's this couple from Girth & Mirth that take their shirts off and they're not ashamed, and they try to make me feel comfortable doing the same.

Interestingly, raising this big man's confidence comes at a cost. It is done by privileging tops over bottoms and thus reinforcing heteronormative gender role stereotypes as they relate to sexual expectations of the "real" man who initiates sex, while the feminized man, or the woman, receives it. At the same time, the club provides a friendly, social environment where there is no pressure to have sex. In this shame-free zone, members feel encouraged to get comfortable in their own skin.

Girth & Mirth's supportive network allows big gay men to revel in the same pleasures other body types of gay men get to experience. At the club's charity bar night, which is held at the Bear bar, gay big men are able to behave freely in ways they most likely could not at gay circuit parties—where the majority of men with ideal body types would be confident enough to dance around on the stage shirtless. The following excerpt from my fieldnotes at bar night illustrates big men's comfort with dancing in a fat-affirming context.

Girth & Mirth members sit on stools by the entrance between the main bar and the DJ booth, watching videos, taking the $2 cover, ogling incoming guests, and trying to talk over the hissing smoke machine. The club is filling up quickly, but the dance floor is empty, since it's still early in the night. Back by the lounge bar, three big men coax one another to get out there. The biggest (and by appearance youngest) of the three begins stripping off layers of clothing. One by one, he pulls off a leather vest, shirt, and then undershirt. One of the other men follows suit and lifts up his t-shirt. Before long, they are both moving their bellies sensually together under a red and amber strobe—bumpin' 'n' grindin' bare bellies on the dance floor, smiling and having fun. In the safe space of Girth & Mirth's bar night, the two dancers make their fat bellies boldly visible, rather than shamefully trying to conceal them.

This bumping of bellies on the dance floor is reminiscent of the "fat handshake" I witnessed at a pop culture conference, where fat activist Wann concluded a meeting by asking those present to face one another and bump their stomachs together before leaving. At another Girth & Mirth charity bar night, I witnessed the same leave-taking ritual between a club member and the new bar manager, a big man himself. The two men had not seen each other since high school and spent most of the night catching up. At the end of the evening when they were bidding farewell to each other, they moved in close and cheerfully rubbed their bellies together.

Members also develop further strategies to increase newcomers' level of body comfort and sexual assertiveness. The following excerpt from my fieldnotes refers to attempts by Girth & Mirthers to get big, and usually younger, men to loosen up. Oftentimes, this involves encouraging them to shed protective layers of clothing, as though letting go of a hangup with each layer:

> A young man in his early twenties, short and chubby, well-groomed and -dressed, wearing glasses, enters the bar. He has on an awful lot of layers for coming out to a club. He holds his body stiffly and hovers around those of us working the door. Some of the men take him under their wing, talk him up, and compliment his features. He proceeds to get tongue-tied, his face flushes, and he tugs at his collar, saying, "It's hot in here." He tells us he went shopping today and spent $400 on new clothes. The guys urge him to take off his zip-up sweater, which he does. Now, he fusses for a long time with his new J.Crew button-up shirt. He nervously pulls at and fidgets with its hem, fluffing the clinging shirt out away from his stomach and his sides, and then smoothing it out again. Later, group members persuade him to unbutton his collar. He is wearing yet another t-shirt underneath. The main doorkeeper lifts the young man's t-shirt up a bit and rubs his fat belly. He continues to hang out with us the rest of the night.

The Girth & Mirthers' attempts at building up this shy visitor are similar to how, at a big men's weekend event, a club member announced guests coming into the hospitality room by rolling out the red carpet, so to speak, as if they were all VIPs. In this way, the doorman celebrated each man's appearance, no matter what his body type was.

Gaining Visibility at Pride

As club members have said, "Girth & Mirth is about being big and loving it." It is about wide pride versus internalizing the outside criticism of being obese. On some fundamental level, celebrating the fat body can be good for one's mental health, and the first step is to enjoy and value oneself as a big gay man.

At a Girth & Mirth Pride-planning meeting, members came to the club's defense in response to a chatroom attack. The online attackers called them an "embarrassment to the gay community" and even suggested they "disband," arguing, "We shouldn't encourage large people." During our meeting, one member gave his opinion of the situation. He figuratively got on his soapbox, exclaiming, "We're robust! Some people missin' some social skills to mingle with people!" He continued his fat rant, saying,

> Bears are "normal," and Girth & Mirthers are not? Chubs have let themselves go? We go out there and have the courage to be who we are. Some people clap, some laugh at us, and some laugh with us. The point is we're being noticed by riding in the parade. We are positive role models with a message: "You can be big and still find people who will like you for it." You know, Bears are also looked at with revulsion. People say, "Get a razor, would it kill you to shave your back?" Then they say we don't look normal. They'll titter at you. Some people internalize it, but you can't do that. Don't apologize for being who you are. Speak out! We're out there doing our thing and we're happy with ourselves.

Another member chimed in with "I concur, that's healthy," while the feisty orator finished by saying, "Snorting cocaine and taking an hour and a half to get ready is not being who you are. It's not like any of us are born with glitter on our faces!"

In this fat rant, the speaker shifted the blame to another group, negatively evaluating what he saw as the hard-partying lives of those caught up in the gay circuit—amid drugs, covered in glitter—and he criticized their body worship and obsession with physical appearance. However, it seems this speaker's fat pride comes at the expense of glammed-up club kids whom he pigeonholes as all being cokeheads, raving the night away in a state of delirium. Gresham Sykes and David Matza refer to this blame-shifting as "condemnation of the [imagined] condemners," a technique of neutralization through which people deflect shame when they believe they have done nothing wrong.[9] Nevertheless, he offers other options to gay men, having to do with feeling good about their bodies and sexual orientation. His polemic resignifies what it means to be gay and healthy, as he equates health with being big and happy rather than with being appearance-obsessed and coked out. He also redefines what it means to be "who you are" when he upholds being ursine over vain. He offers what Judith (Jack) Halberstam optimistically refers to as a "total disregard for shame and its tortuous pathways."[10]

Girth & Mirthers' participation in the Pride parade created a stir, so to speak; they did not cause any trouble, but their presence encouraged those on the sidelines to do body talk,[11] especially about size, a different issue from sexuality—though as I have argued throughout, taken together, their size and sexual orientation amplify marginalization. At the first Pride parade I attended as a participant observer, I marched at the head of the Girth & Mirth procession, holding one end of the club's banner. Also up front was someone carrying the American flag, while others walked waving their Bear flags. Puzzled onlookers read the banner aloud and said, "Girth & Mirth?" Then they either would exclaim, "What's that?" or would laugh. A guy holding a sign in support of normalizing gay marriage shouted, "He's anorexic!" targeting me, meaning who was I to represent the group? One of the flagbearers saved me and came back with, "He's the mirth!" With this flippant remark, he nipped in the bud the negative body talk. And despite all the snickering, a lot of people did cheer for the group. For instance, a woman on the sidelines clapped and yelled, "Big daddies!"

For some members, being in the Pride parade meant they came out for two separate vectors of identity: for being gay and for being fat; or, as in the case of a chaser, for being gay and for being a fat-admirer. A chub I interviewed volunteered a story about a Pride parade he attended in which he and a chaser were hamming it up as they marched, while his chubby partner also played along. He said the onlookers dramatically covered their mouths and exclaimed in a fit of feigned horror, "Oh, my God!" He continued to elaborate that although their display was deliberately provocative, it put a face to Girth & Mirth members as being a fun-loving bunch.

> We were walking without our shirts on, literally just in rainbow towels for the five-mile parade route. Our chaser would rub our bellies and say, "It's all about the belly, baby!" It was hot, and we were sweaty, and he would be out there kissing our bellies and everything. People would just laugh, but he got off on it and it was fun and it represented to the public who we are and what we're all about.

Similarly, in a *San Francisco Bay Times* article the author quips tongue-in-cheek on the sterilization of Pride: "The Girth & Mirth club will be asked to either not be fat or at least not show a sense of humor about their stout state. After all, we wouldn't want the public to think that a bunch of happy, chubby gays represented our community, now would we?!"[12] The author of this article affectionately acknowledges the existence of big men in the gay community. His remarks underscore the contradiction that if gays are open to making fun of themselves via being comedic drag queens and engaging in campy behavior, they should not be so threatened by Girth & Mirthers' being part of the gay community.

As Probyn argues, shame is a socially interactive process that requires the shamers and their victims to be in close proximity. It is "a particularly visceral sensation."[13] Girth & Mirthers feel shame for falling short of the ideal gay image even more acutely when their shamers are gays themselves. When they participate in Pride celebrations, they not only gain visibility, but they also offer onlookers an alternate image. As one big man told me, "I think we as a group at Pride have tried to show that not all gays are pretty-perfect, chiseled guys. We are who we are. We accept who we are. We know we're not society's ideal of physical perfection. We're big guys, we have fun, and we're okay with it." Girth & Mirthers march in Pride parades, dispelling any preconceived notions others may hold of what body types constitute the "gay community." The Pride parade also provides an avenue for connecting with the larger society. However, to the extent that the Girth & Mirthers' presence in the parade causes a ruckus, it magnifies their shame.

Thus, visibility does not always translate to social acceptance. As Suzanna Walters has shown in her book *All the Rage: The Story of Gay Visibility in America*, the correlation between increased visibility in mainstream society and social acceptance is not so clear.[14] Likewise, I problematize the fantasy of making progress from visibility toward integration. Furthermore, the case of Girth & Mirthers poses a different problem. Because big gay men feel the sting of exclusion especially from gay society, my argument is not a question of mainstream acceptance of big gay men. Given their ample size, the more visible big men are, the more the gay community overlooks them. In other words, rather than remain imprisoned in the closet because of societal judgment of their sexual orientation, big men are isolated and imprisoned by the gay community's judgment of their size.

According to Goffman, a stigmatized individual who wants public approval needs to adopt "the right line."[15] Only then will he have "come to terms with himself and be a whole man . . . an adult with dignity and respect."[16] Goffman's "right line" was illustrated well in the second Pride parade I attended, where the big men unexpectedly came in first place for their float theme, "Rub-a-dub-dub, Big Men in a Tub." The men rode in a larger-than-life bathtub replete with shower curtains that blew gently as the truck moved along the parade route. The tub was overflowing with Girth & Mirthers, whom I joined, as we all blew bubbles at the onlookers. The big men indeed had adopted an acceptable party line by playing into others' stereotype of them as jolly fat men.

Festival occasions bring out the best in Girth & Mirthers, as they offer a perfect venue for playing around with multiple signifiers. The rub-a-dub-dub theme was successful, as it was open to interpretation. First, there is simply the mirthful rub-a-dub-dubbing. Then, the theme invokes an innocent nursery rhyme; and third, it alludes to homosexuality, because three men are in a tub together. At the same time, because the float is based on such an innocent nursery rhyme, some observers may miss the sexual overtone altogether, which would mean that the big men end up infantilizing themselves. The big men's playing with signifiers lives up to LeBesco's call for fat politics to begin engaging in ever more playful subjectivity and performativity.[17] Bear groups had tested this bubble-bath theme before in other Pride parades, and it had been equally successful. In the case of both clubs using the rub-a-dub-dub theme, they are not making a desperate attempt to normalize; rather, they open up the signifiers to multiple interpretations in order to counteract knee-jerk reactions to fat.

Consumer Inclusion within the Gay Community

Another form of resistance in which Girth & Mirthers engage is consumer complaint, as in the case of one member's letter to the Human Rights Campaign (HRC) regarding its lack of extended sizes in gay rights t-shirts. I learned about this man's letter of concern briefly expressing his displeasure with HRC when he told a group of us about it at a spring pot-luck. He later forwarded it to me. As he wrote in his letter,

This is not a concern about an order that has been placed, but rather about an order that *cannot* be placed. HRC is a great organization, but by offering t-shirts that only go up to size 2X, it is excluding a large (no pun intended) section of the gay community. It would be nice if HRC would offer t-shirts in larger sizes for those of us that do not fit the perfect-body stereotype.

There is a fundamental flaw in the system to which this letter points. While the HRC organizational logo on a t-shirt represents gay solidarity, some Girth & Mirthers cannot fit into shirts that stop at size 2X. The HRC, whose mission is to work toward equal rights for the LGBT community, has thus committed a serious oversight in not taking into account part of the very population it is organized to protect.

The idea of "peaceful consumer revolution" has been introduced by LeBesco, who sees it as a move toward assimilation.[18] In my study, the act of supporting organizations that make clothing inclusive of all sizes and opposing those that do not represents such a revolutionary act. The HRC letter-writing example is a peaceful attempt to bring a gay organization in line with big men's clothing needs. Returning to the political potential of Girth & Mirth, LeBesco's framing device for the politics of size is fitting here as one of compromised victories and pleasures.[19] For example, the Casual Male fashion show at Convergence is a compromised victory, because it still buys into the fashion industry, the same industry that excludes people of size. Yet, creating a chain for big and tall men's clothing is no small feat. Arguably, it would be even *more* revolutionary for fat people to alter clothes from stores that accommodate plus sizes, thus defying the "tasteful" intent of the original design.[20] For example, the ability to take big swim trunks and cut out the mesh to make oneself more accessible for fondling in the pool at the Cabana was definitely not the intent of the makers of those stylish shorts.

Fat gay shame opens up the possibility for overlapping agendas with other underrepresented groups like female fat activists. The letter to HRC is in fact consistent with strategies that the National Association to Advance Fat Acceptance uses in contesting shame.[21] The letter writer's pointing out a group excluded from the shame-to-pride conversion process because of its members' body shape and size closely resembles how "gay shame can be used . . . in ways that are feminist" in challenging social injustice.[22]

One way to stave off shame is to blame the system. According to Britt and Heise, "[S]ocial movements provide justification for making an attribution about the system rather than the self . . . not only because the system is unjust, but [because people are] angry that they have been made to feel ashamed."[23] Consumer complaint poses questions about niche recognition and the role fat people play in the marketplace. It underscores the impact of being recognized as a fat consumer. How does fat people's wanting to be acknowledged as valuable customers factor into the way they organize as activists? When one lodges all of one's grievances in consumerism, then, presumably all of one's problems would be solved as soon as manufacturers and corporations addressed them. However, this is when it is important to consider how fat identity is cemented. Buying shirts from HRC is a way to conspicuously consume conformist gay identity. When big men wish they could fit into those shirts with the HRC logo, they are really desperately seeking a share in something that other gays are enjoying and are not necessarily being all that radical. They are simply engaging in a negative transvaluation of the ideal gay male body. Declining to associate with gay men who pursue the "perfect body" allows big men to rise above organizational and community rejection so that they do not sink into self-rejection.

While it is difficult enough to find clothes in mainstream society that fit one's larger body, it becomes even more of a challenge when Girth & Mirthers want to shop at a trendy gay boutique. It is rare, for example, to find in such stores t-shirts that come in sizes 2-3-4X. Consequently, as big men have remarked, they like to support vendors that are thoughtful enough to carry gay apparel in extended sizes. Girth & Mirthers intentionally patronize these establishments. One member described his sometimes overdoing it, stocking up when he finds gay-themed apparel in his size.

> This past year at Pride, it was funny. I bought several t-shirts. I got the Stonewall Pride t-shirt, only because it came in my size. And if a gay organization offers t-shirts for fundraising or whatever, and has something in my size, I'm gonna buy it. Because if they had the forethought to include a person of size, male or female, I'm gonna buy it. For the True Colors tour, the t-shirts only went up to 2XL. And they were small 2XLs. I was upset. But this year at Pride, I had a couple of opportunities to buy t-shirts, and I bought them because they were available. And people in the club were saying, "Why? What's going on?" And I said, "It's my size, it's a gay organization, I'm gonna buy it." If they're gonna be thoughtful enough to think there might be somebody big out there, I'm gonna buy the shirt.

Given the focus on fashion in gay society, when big men are denied the latest clothing trends they miss out on the opportunity to be like their gay peers. Therefore, big men like to funnel their dollars into gay businesses that provide them with more options in clothing. They do not necessarily denounce gay fashionistas, but rather make an appeal for stylish big men's clothing. That is, they are not opposed to gay fashion but simply want a corner of its market, their desire for inclusion creating strange bedfellows.

Differentiating Fat

Big men have consistently bewailed the problem of the lack of differentiation imposed on all fat people. They resist the reductionist belief that there is nothing more to them beyond their size, and they are invested in reclaiming their right to self-definition. Therefore, they make an effort to set themselves apart through complimentary portrayals of their bodies or redirect attention away from their fatness by normalizing it, so that other attributes can be recognized. One Girth

& Mirther distinguishes himself as a talented artist. As he said, being an artist defines him:

> It is one of the things that I like to do, and people say I do it well. It's a way for me to be different, and on the vain side, it offers an excuse for me to be a little bit weird. I can always say, "Well, I'm an artist." I can wear these clothes, I can do this, and I can say these off-the-wall things and behave a little bit, you know, kicky and weird. It gives me another opportunity to be known for that, so people can say, "Oh, we have an artist in our group." I use that as a tool to support the club, which I've done now with the newsletter and helping design the Pride parade float—I've been enlisted to come up with some graphics for that.

This Girth & Mirther also spoke about using club members as models for a series of five paintings he called *Gods and Magic* that "uphold the larger male form as something to be admired, as opposed to something to be ridiculed." He believed doing so would enable him and the models to remedy the weak existing imagery of big men by producing realistic images of them: "It won't be the thin, muscular bodies; they'll be club guys, big guys, with all the hanging fat if it's there. It's the body type I want in these pictures." This big gay artist went on to say that three people from Girth & Mirth have already posed for him so that he could do some sketches. His depictions of big men's bodies cast him alongside artists throughout history, from photographs by Leonard Nimoy, whose *Full Body Project* depicts big women in black and white, to Rubenesque art, to the primitive *Venus of Willendorf* statues. He is in fact further differentiated from these artists, in that his art will bring the invisible fat man to the fore.

LeBesco talks about how the slogan "Big Is Beautiful" is misleading; big is not necessarily beautiful in all instances, but it still is normal and deserves unexceptional treatment.[24] Therefore, the artist above who strives to make fat bodies admirable and godlike in his paintings might do better to paint them as ordinary mortals. At the same time, this big man succeeds in differentiating himself as an artist, which itself is a mark of making progress toward a self-concept that is multidimensional and less limiting. His claiming the identity of artist defies what shamers do when they reduce big men solely to their size.

Big men differentiate themselves by different kinds of body excesses, such as by wearing fat-revealing and provocative dress, or by acknowledging their body size through artistic renditions. Traditionally, masculinity also affords options for dealing with body excess; it differentiates size by genitals or, more commonly, through muscles and bodybuilding. While the artist I discuss above renders fat hypervisible in his paintings, some big men who go to Bear bars differentiate themselves by foregrounding other attributes, like a larger-than-life personality or their sexual prowess. Thus, fat is not the overriding identity marker, as it is in the works of art. One big man put it this way about going to the Bear bar during Girth & Mirth's charity bar night:

> A lot of men go in there and let their bellies hang out. It's not uncommon to see guys without their shirts on who have a big paunch. It's just nice to be around, to be in a place where you're not going to be judged by your size, but by your personality, or your dick, or your sexual interests, not just your belly.

Because many people at the Girth & Mirth bar night are big, men's ample size gets established as a baseline, so that they are able to focus on and accentuate other aspects of themselves. When big men can move beyond being evaluated by their body shape and size, they are finally able to be "regular guys," who perseverate over "guy things" like their penis size.

Performing Shame and Celebrating Otherness

Big gay men respond to everyday shame through outrageous and performative acts, as illustrated in chapter 3. Going beyond daily survival and demanding a "livable life,"[25] they revel in their body size and celebrate their "otherness" as they engage in campy-queer performances. As Sedgwick writes, "[S]hame/performativity may get us a lot further with the cluster of phenomena generally called 'camp.'"[26] Big men engage in campy, self-critical acts in an effort to reframe an identity produced by the stigma surrounding their size. Using drag as her example, Halberstam prefers to think of taking pride in one's shame as going to "a place where shame can be transformed into something that is not pride, but not simply damage, either."[27]

The following excerpt from my fieldnotes, written after working with the Girth & Mirth fellows at a Halloween Bar Night, illustrates how one member took pride in his shame.

I am wearing an official Boy Scout hat and shirt: a self-presentation strategy that became awkward after a former Scout criticized my costume concept. A big, monumental fat couple is also in costume tonight. I sit at the entrance with these men, welcoming guests and collecting cover charges most of the evening.

The main doorperson works the register and calls his costume idea "Catch of the Day." He is shirtless. He wears an old pair of yellow rubber fisherman's overalls with one strap dangling; the other is a marvelous sash made of fishing net and finished with fancy fake fish and assorted seafood. His costume design reveals his fat chest and midriff. Wispy white hairs billow out the back of his low-cut overalls and his bald head bears no fisherman's cap.

To his credit, Catch of the Day has managed to rise above the notion that the only acceptable appearance is one that is altered. He has neither tried to conceal his fat body nor tamed his hirsute shoulders; he is not covering up his hair loss, either. However, it would be a mistake to interpret Catch of the Day's costume concept literally as some broader critique of the ideal body.

Aside from my Scout costume, no one on that Halloween bar night was taking anything literally. These men live far from any fishing communities, as Provincetown on Cape Cod used to be, which is now a gay Mecca. The fisherman in overalls was meant to be about a big and middle-aged man being a good catch. Indeed, his boyfriend had already caught, and intended to keep, him. Despite his costume's strong connection to a masculine identity construction, his outfit is not meant to be taken seriously to suggest a truly rugged, adventurous, weathered, scruffy fisherman. His parody is campy and artificial, and it shows the constructed nature of the fisherman's role. It differs from gay Bears' attire; their masculine, working-class, or lumberjack drag is a turn-on. Leo Bersani's passing remark seems relevant here: "Parody is an erotic turn-off and all gay men know this. . . . [W]hile that may be fun at a dinner party, if you're out to make someone [really horny], you turn off the camp."[28]

Catch of the Day explained the reasons why he felt it necessary to go all out in creating his costume. He said he felt that in order to gain visibility as a big gay man and to put a face to Girth & Mirth, he had to go to extremes in presenting a fun, larger-than-life persona.

> I have days when I don't care what people think and I'm gonna do what I want. If somebody doesn't like it, they can kiss my ass. And then there are days when I'm like, Okay, we're going out in public, and we have to be publicly acceptable. The more we as a community push the envelope, even when we're in our own spaces, the more we're out in public and we're doing things, the more accepting people will be, and they'll say, "Oh, those people look like they're having a good time." And to show that, you have to be a little more extreme. You have to be larger than life, or you're just not gonna be noticed, 'cause there are so many people who are larger than life, you know? In the gay community, part of how we're getting more accepted in society as a whole is to be a little extreme.

Catch of the Day certainly made a splash with his over-the-top costume. His efforts to gain visibility indeed did not go unnoticed.

Sedgwick proposes going further than Goffman in his book *Stigma*.[29] As she suggests, it would be good to expand Goffman's subtitle, *Notes on the Management of Spoiled Identity*, to include more than just identity management, because, in any queer politics, one also approaches one's spoiled identity in ways that are "experimental, creative, performative."[30] In this sense, Catch of the Day's in-your-face largeness is a defiant act carried out in the company of other gay men, whose acceptance-tolerance-rejection may indeed hinge on how he has put himself together.

Those with a body out of bounds can also use laughter to disrupt shame. According to Thomas Scheff, this is healthier than unacknowledged shame.[31] One member of Girth & Mirth, who had a fat drag queen for a roommate, tells a story about how she busted out laughing, literally from her corset, when he compared her preparation for her show to a scene from *Gone with the Wind*.

> My old roommate, a fat drag queen, ordered a fishbone corset. One night before her show, she summoned me to help coax her body into an hourglass figure. I wrestled her into the tight-laced corset. And while I was yanking her in, it reminded me of that scene from *Gone with the Wind* between Scarlett O'Hara and her mammy. I said, "I guess you have to resign yourself to havin' a 20-inch waist instead of 18 inches like it was before the baby, oh, fiddle dee dee!" We both broke out laughing so hard, her brand new corset split!

By letting loose the restrictions around her waistline, this queen is filled with generous, good-natured humor. Scheff makes a distinction between shying away from shame and lightheartedly dismissing it. He writes, "One method which almost always dispels shame is laughter, good-humored or affectionate laughter. This idea is very much in accord with the popular belief [that] laughter relieves embarrassment," thereby disrupting shame.[32]

The penultimate example of Girth & Mirth's playful disregard of shame is Bearilyn's Birthday Wish, which uses camp to celebrate a big man's birthday. Bearilyn, as the group affectionately calls him, aestheticizes shame through a parody of the song Marilyn Monroe sang to President John F.

Kennedy in 1962, "Happy Birthday, Mr. President." He has made it his mission to recognize people's birthdays in this manner. Bearilyn combines the birthday song with a lapdance for the unlucky birthday boy of the night, be it at the Italian restaurant Spaghetti Warehouse or at the coffee house.

Voluptuous like Marilyn, Bearilyn exudes a healthy sexuality with his full figure. He does Marilyn moves and copies her playful hip wiggle that made her a star. In an interview, one of his friends described Bearilyn as follows:

> He is not one of the most masculine guys, but he's a guy. But when he lets his hair down, he does this thing for birthdays. I mean, oh my God, it brings the house down wherever we are. He's a big guy and he uses what he has, to be Marilyn Monroe, rubbing somebody's head and putting it between his boobs and it's just, you have to see it, if it was videoed, you would die.[33]

Asking the lucky recipient to sit on a chair with plenty of space around it, Bearilyn lapdances as he sings in breathy, low-pitched vocals. Having seen this performance on numerous occasions and even been treated to it once on my own birthday, I would reiterate it as follows:

♪ HAPPY—BIRTH-DAY . . .
(Sensually caresses the birthday boy's head, neck, and chest)
♪ TO YOU,
(Unbuttons the birthday boy's collar and undoes his own to show some cleavage)
♪ HAPPY—BIRTH-DAY . . .
(Grabs recipient by the neck)
♪ TO YOU
(Pushes the birthday boy's face into his ample chest; breast-shaking action ensues)
♪ HAPPY—BIRTH-DAY . . .
(Sits on the birthday boy's lap facing away; leans head back on his shoulder)

♪ MR. PRES-I-DENT
(Sits upright and wiggles his derrière on the birthday boy's lap)
♪ HAPPY—BIRTH-DAY . . .
(Stands up and pulls open the birthday boy's collar)
♪ TO
(Pulls the birthday boy's head tightly against his chest)
♪♪ YOU
(Guides the birthday boy's mouth onto his nipple)

As his song ends, Bearilyn bends over and whispers to the recipient, "Thank you ever so." In many ways, this one-man show is comparable to the political actions that some fat women's groups take, because it challenges stereotypes of what is "sexy" and "beautiful." For example, there is the California-based Big Burlesque (later renamed the Fat Bottom Revue) and PHAT Fly Girls. Then, there is the radical cheerleading group Fat Action Troupe All-Star Spirit Squad (F.A.T.A.S.S.). These women's groups refer to what they do as "creative activism." Their goal is to empower the audience because they can see and appreciate size diversity—maybe someone who actually looks like them. When Bearilyn performs the birthday song, he too empowers his audience of big men by being sexy and suggestive, lewd and bawdy.

The boldness and confidence Bearilyn's performance exudes is summed up best in the words of the late Heather MacAllister (a.k.a. Reva Lucian): "Anytime there is a fat person onstage as anything besides the butt of a joke, it's political. Add physical movement, then dance, then sexuality, and you have a revolutionary act."[34] Indeed, Bearilyn's performance is not demure; it does not represent a recoiling from shame or trying to blend into body-perfect gay society; on the contrary, it flaunts the limits and resists "normal" representations of fatness through the comic mayhem of neo-burlesque.

As Bearilyn himself has remarked, his birthday song is about making someone feel recognized on his special day. He credits the origin of this performance to his husband's mother:

When I was at my mother-in-law's house in Florida, she said: "Oh, you have another birthday coming up pretty soon." I made the mistake of saying, "Birthdays are just another day, they're no big deal." She replied, "Yes, they are! Your birthday is your day. You have to share all the holidays, but your birthday is *your* day. It's important." So ever since then, I try to make my husband's birthday important, and I try to make my birthday important, and I try to make everybody else's important, too.

Bearilyn's performance epitomizes the campy-queer respite the club offers. Humor, in the campy-queen sense, is a weapon for freedom fighting, as well. Big men who find themselves down on their luck can count on members like Bearilyn to come along and lift their spirits. Much of what Girth & Mirthers do for one another, as they told me, is, "when a person finds himself in a bad situation, or they just had a streak of bad luck, we'll step up to the plate and do or say something to lift them up a little." Shame is often experienced as vulnerability, but here, that same experience translates into playful physical activity, or even titillation.

One member of Girth & Mirth who is into S&M equated Bearilyn's kind of campy humor that one finds at the club with tickle-torture: "Hopefully, you're not ticklish because humor—the capping,[35] the puns— is equivalent to me tying you down and tickle-torturing you for the next hour. You can have a lot of fun with it."

As other group members have remarked, Bearilyn serves as a mascot for Girth & Mirth, and his playful spirit rubs off. The Girth & Mirther above also talked about the contagious effect of Bearilyn's lapdance, which he was moved to emulate.

On the night of the Girth & Mirth pot-luck at my house, my neighbor next door was having a birthday party. After she blew out the candles, they accidentally dropped the cake. When I found out, I brought them a big chunk of our Chocolate Death by Brownie dessert. I asked her to sit in a chair, straddled her, and did the Happy Birthday routine, Marilyn Monroe–style. And then I pulled the bowl of cake around in front of me and everybody thought I was gonna smash it in her face, but I took it and gently fed it to her while I sang "Happy Birthday." Then, I ran my finger down her neck and toward her breasts. I didn't grope her, you know, she's a woman, I don't want that.

So, a part of Bearilyn rubbed off on me. And that is a lot of what Girth & Mirth will do.

The Bearilyn song is a food-informed event, as when the speaker above shared a chunk of chocolate brownie with his next-door neighbor in Marilynesque fashion. Food can integrate people into the community, serving as a unifying element in celebrations, gay or otherwise. It can thus help to mute the shame of fat stigma. The Chocolate Death by Brownie described by the big man above provided a link between club members and their neighbors in the local community. Additionally, whenever Bearilyn performs the birthday song at a kaffeeklatsch, all eyes are on him. During such occasions, Girth & Mirthers experience what it feels like to be the center of attention.

Another Girth & Mirther, reflecting on Bearilyn, spoke of how much he appreciates that people can be who they want to be at club activities and some do not have to put on the "butch" act when they are around one another. He remarked that at the club, they can let their hair down.

The club is a place where, if you have to butch it up at work, and you have to butch it up for the neighbors, and you have to butch it up to go to the grocery, well then, God dammit, there's got to be a place where you can go where you don't have to butch it up, and if you want to queen out, or get campy, or whatever, Mary,[36] you can just do it.

Indeed, members regard Girth & Mirth as their home away from home, a place where they can go and simply nurture joy. The club also helps members own and name the stigma of being fat and celebrate their otherness. Some members come to use a transvaluative strategy to reconfigure their shame and transform the abjectness they feel into something desirable.[37]

This is not to say that Girth & Mirthers necessarily set out to reconfigure their shame or to challenge injustice. They remain ambivalent, or, at
most, they simply manage within the status quo, normalize their "deviant
identity," and come to accept and be at ease with their size.[38]

Conclusion

Beyond Simply Managing Stigma

Herein, I have thickly described some of the ways in which big gay men have reconfigured the shame of fat stigma, either by turning themselves into sex objects (the focus of chapter 3), or by seeking class validation (the focus of chapter 4), or by playfully disregarding their shame (the focus of chapter 5). Typically, people reconfigure fat as a disease or deviance, such as when doctors medicalize it as "obesity" or when people say someone is "overweight," meaning he has deviated from some ideal measurement. Big men, however, have devised different strategies for reconfiguring the shame of fat stigma. My investigation into the activities of Girth & Mirthers showed while some may turn themselves into sex objects, their reconfiguration of fat shame is not always reduced to their sexual behavior; it can also be done through their level of outness about their size, status symbols, or consumer inclusion, as well as by reclaiming the right to self-definition or by taking shelter among their big brethren at a coffee house, club pot-luck, or weekend retreat.

As I reflect on what I have learned during my fieldwork among the Girth & Mirthers, I am reminded of one particular response to the final interview question I asked the participants: "In wrapping up, is there anything you expected me to ask or you wanted to share that I did not cover?" A couple I interviewed asked me in return what I *myself* had to add at this point. One of them inquired, "As a newcomer to our club and as a person who is doing this survey, what are *your* observations and how has this research changed *your* thoughts on, or image of, bigger people?" And his partner added, "That's exactly what I was going to ask you earlier, and then I realized if you were a researcher worth half your weight in gold, you wouldn't answer that question until you got done."

Indeed, over the course of time I spent with the Girth & Mirthers, many insights and observations slowly came to me. For example, I saw how, in ever so minute increments, the big men's acts of courage locally and out of town seemed to build on one another, and their over-the-top antics and outrageous behavior when away from their home turf did leave a residue of empowerment. This argument can be a tough sell, however. Readers of earlier drafts of my work have commented that the big men's attempts at sexualizing away from home at the weekend retreats amount to merely fleeting repairs of their wounded identities. The readers have questioned whether such reconfigurations truly get to the heart of the matter or whether they are just sad fixes. They point out the reality that the big men themselves know all too well: They still have to leave the weekend retreats and return to homophobic mainstream society and especially to fatphobic gay society. However, I have witnessed distinct carryovers from the weekend retreats to the big men's behavior locally. Taking over the motel for the duration of the Super Weekend and Bearilyn's performing his birthday song are indeed examples of out-of-town retreats and local events that are mutually reinforcing. And these acts have a cumulative effect; they build on one another to give big gay men the wherewithal to weather their shame.

I also saw that it takes enormous courage for gay big men to engage in campy-queer behaviors or march in the Pride parade and put themselves out there, when they acutely feel the sting of being unwelcome by gay men of "normal" body builds. I witnessed that for big gay men, coming out as a form of reconfiguring the shame of fat stigma involves different types of disclosures—coming out as fat is different from coming out as gay. A fat person does not *exactly* "come out" of the closet. Then again, there are choices one makes in performing one's fat identity: Should one pose nude in a magazine, flab and all, making fat pride about owner-ship? Should one perform fat burlesque in a mainstream coffee house? Or march alongside his fellow Girth & Mirthers in the Pride parade? These are all courageous choices; walking down the street with a group of other big men in a Pride parade is not just about managing one's stigma—it takes courage.

In reaction to being treated as a single undifferentiated mass, big men engage in performances of reconfiguring the shame of their fat stigma by differentiating their myriad fat selves from hackneyed essentialist stereotypes. One such resignification of fat is to declare that big is beau-tiful. This strategy, too, makes big men objects of desire in a subculture where they are also permitted to be desiring subjects. When the artist decided to make the paintings of big men, for instance, he was doing it out of admiration for their form. Yet another way big men try to differ-entiate fat from reductionist stereotypes is to masculinize it and make an authenticity claim as to who is the "real" gay man: the fat, hairy guy with a healthy appetite, or the anorectic, drugged-out circuit gay? Big men would like nothing better than to lay claim to being championed as the *real* gay men.

Reconfiguring one's shame also requires acts of humility. To gain vis-ibility, Girth & Mirthers willingly carry the torch of public humility, as they do when they walk in the Pride parade and suffer the humiliation of not only the usual remarks from religious protesters but also sizist remarks from heterosexual homophobes; and worse, they suffer snick-ering from gays. And it is the last of these, the within-group injury, that hurts the most. Even when gay big men manage to reconfigure their shame, they can never completely eradicate it. The shaming is a slap in the face, coming mostly from their own identity group. There also is the question of whom the big men choose to be the audience for their per-formances. It appears that at the Pride parade, gay big men shake up the gay scene, whereas at the Super Weekend's carnivalesque events, they are good-humoredly thumbing their noses at themselves, and not so much at others in the gay community.

Many contradictions are not resolved in this book. For instance, the normative world that gay chubs must navigate is in opposition to a world in which chasers have more latitude. It is also true that some chubs want to be desired by chasers who string them along, which falls right in line with one of the paradoxes of love: People desire the person who plays hard to get or, at its extreme, the person who abuses them.[1] Another unresolved tension is that some chubs want to be a part of the gay fashion scene, the same one that excludes them. Petitioning for consumer inclusion is among Girth & Mirthers' efforts to reconfigure, but when big men point out that they have been left out of fashion consumerism, they are buying into the very system that overlooked them.[2]

Thus, the concept of strange bedfellows is important here. While contradictions remain, they seem to coexist without much ado, regardless of whether they make sense. I have tried to be careful to celebrate the tensions, rather than assume the task of resolving them. For example, it is a little ironic that to seek social acceptance, Girth & Mirthers do some rather socially unacceptable things during their weekend reunions. Instead of trying to make heads or tails of such a paradox, I have been interested in identifying the tensions among all of the players in this book, or between their motives and strategies.

Finally, a question open for debate is, "Which big men's reunion addresses their wounds better?" In disrupting the signifiers, the big men's play at the Super Weekend might be more grassroots. And maybe Convergence does not do as good a job of disrupting the signifiers. Such an argument would accord more power to the carnival event at the Super Weekend than to the classier event at Convergence. Then again, if attendance is a useful measure, Convergence always draws a larger crowd than the Super Weekend and therefore must offer big men something meaningful. The cultural activities at Convergence may resonate more with the ordinary lives of big gay men than the annual Super Weekend's carnival. Likewise, the Super Weekend, in all of its uncomfortable forms of shapeshifting, may lead to a significant paradigm revolution for many big men who attend. Overall, both Convergence and the Super Weekend are valuable, as each offers different strategies for addressing big gay men's social injuries.

This ethnography of Girth & Mirth culture provides a smorgasbord of strategies for dealing with the shame of fat stigma. Despite their unfortunate tendency to internalize shame and allow it to run their lives, big men continue to find more productive outlets, such as sexual objectification, status differentiation, and celebrating otherness. One of my own personal favorites is campy-queer performances that utterly disregard shame, playfully acknowledging one's size in relation to one's sexuality. What a burden it is to be stigmatized; and what an admirable feat to perform one's way out of the isolation of being stigmatized. Undoubtedly, the road to acceptance appears to be paved with something *more* than simply managing stigma; it requires an unforgettable performance.

METHODOLOGICAL APPENDIX

In writing this book I relied mostly on fieldnotes, which I supplemented with in-depth interviews. Between the fall of 2006 and the fall of 2008, I spent a great deal of time with the local Ohio chapter of Girth & Mirth. I attended more than one hundred events, interacting with the big men at bar nights, kaffeeklatsches, restaurants, pot-luck dinners, holiday bashes, pool parties, and game and movie nights. I also attended weekend retreats that took me outside of Ohio to regional and national events held in Oklahoma and Minnesota. Following the first seventy-five of these events I attended, I converted my field diary into typed notes and elaborated on them with coding schemas and theoretical memos that became the basis for starting my analysis.

After two years, I drew back from regular attendance at group events and started to focus on the writing more, while corresponding with folks via e-mail or phone to ask them to clarify ideas in the passages I was trying to write. From the fall of 2008 to the fall of 2010, I also had lunch every month or two with a key informant, a big man who has served on the club's board as both a longtime treasurer, and most recently webmaster, whom I have come to consider my friend. Today, although the project is completed and I have since moved to a new job across the country, I continue to read messages posted to the group's e-mail discussion list every now and then.

Previous research suggested to me that at social functions the men would distinguish between two broad categories of desire: the desire to experience fraternity and the desire to experience another person's body.[1] Thus, I took fieldnotes on corporeal conduct, such as the way the men used their bodies in certain social contexts. My approach to amassing information about the group was to jot down paper-and-pen notes during, and mostly after, events. Soon afterward, I would type up longer memos.

During my fieldwork, I supplemented my observations and informal interviews with 10 in-depth tape-recorded interviews that produced more than 200 pages of transcript. These formal interviews were voluntary and included a variety of group members, from board members to those who were less involved, as well as from those big men who liked other big men, to two big men who preferred chasers. The interviewees ranged from a married couple, one of whom was an economist with a Ph.D., to an artist who worked at a screen-printing shop. In my interview guide, I included more than 70 questions and possible probes about the body, health, admirers, masculinity, other gay groups, and any negative treatment experienced, and finally I asked about the club's role in the big men's lives. Sometimes I also conducted additional interviews informally through casual conversation. For instance, I would ask a member over a cocktail if he would be willing to clarify ideas I did not understand or to interpret an event for me.

The estimated "active" membership of the local group I studied was approximately twenty to twenty-five. This did not include a fair number of peripheral folks who sporadically showed up. Roughly sixty people subscribed to the club's Yahoo! group and listserv during those first two years of my research, and this online presence has dramatically expanded to include a Facebook page in addition to the group's website. During my research, I witnessed more membership growth than decline. However, because of the small convenient sample, I cannot claim external validity, and local members were largely middle-aged white men. Therefore, the conclusions drawn from this project may not be generalizable to other gay men in similar groups.

Analytical Framework of Stigma, Camp, Carnival, and Play

When I analyzed my data, I used Goffman's stigma theory and extended it by incorporating theories of camp, carnival, play, and performativity. Goffman refers to homosexuals, "gypsies," carnies, prostitutes, and cultists as "social deviants"—people outside the norm who receive differential treatment and are forced to accept their place in society. He discusses how these stigmatized individuals manage their spoiled identities in mixed contact with the "normals." This is not unlike Girth & Mirthers some of the time. As Goffman puts it, interactions between the "normals" and the stigmatized are "one of the primal scenes of sociology."[1] In the case of Girth & Mirthers, they are often put in their place even when they are *not* in mixed company, for their shame is so deeply ingrained. Thus they sometimes tackle their "felt stigma" when performing within their own circuits.

Goffman certainly is interested in the performative actor in relation to stigma; however, he mainly describes social deviants weathering their shame by concealing, covering, managing, passing with it, or taking shelter from it. Today, those working in the sociology of health and illness are trying to deepen our understanding of interactionist stigma theory. They are beginning to see that the personal tragedy (deviance) paradigm has its limitations, as it overlooks elements of social structure—power relations—and fails to challenge unexamined assumptions.[2] Sociologists in tune with what disability scholars have been proposing now think that a social oppression paradigm might be more appropriate, as it is a more politicized approach to stigma. Carol Thomas asserts: "Like feminists and others studying power relations and the social construction of subalterns, writers in disability studies have consistently rejected the social deviance paradigm, turning instead to a social oppression paradigm."[3]

Today, scholars like me have moved beyond Goffman's pioneering efforts in conceptualizing stigma. Graham Scambler writes: "[W]hile Goffman's contribution retains its insight, subtlety and theoretical acuity, it is time to move on, or rather *beyond*: it is not so much that Goffman was wrong, as there were questions he did not ask."[4] For example, conflict theory allows us to ask questions about power relations, while functionalism allows us to explore taken-for-granted assumptions. In this book, I am equally concerned with post-Goffman stigma research into how bodies are shaped by relations of power, or the way(s) social structure shapes how we perceive our bodies. In the functionalist vein, the objective reality of "social facts"[5] regarding body shape and size obscures the possibility of challenging looksism and, particularly relevant to this book, sizism. Scambler talks about the "capacity to fight back" and "resistance and/or defiance."[6] Like Scambler, I am concerned with identity politics. One way he suggests moving beyond the personal tragedy/deviance paradigm is to refine and contextualize the word *stigma* by looking at people who experience co-stigmas. Likewise, Thomas appreciates that "*multiple disadvantage* stalks the social landscape."[7] My work signals a trend toward studying the life worlds of the multiply stigmatized so that the concept of "stigma" can be further refined and contextualized.

At the time Goffman wrote his book *Stigma*, he perhaps could not have anticipated that gays would one day harness power from remaining outside of the norm and would be able to shout out, "We're here, we're queer! Get used to it!" Nor could he foresee fat activists playing off of that and daring to declare, "We're here, we're spheres! Get used to it!"[8] Indeed, Girth & Mirthers offer a positive vision of being both fat and gay, at least in the West. Soon in the United States, being gay will be something completely "normal" and uncontroversial, and at current rates of "obesity," we may all be "obese" before too long, and both of these could really become someone's dream life, or someone else's worst nightmare.

When a group's response to stigma is to play with it, does camp heal stigma? Increasingly, we see academics come to applaud fat activists for their ability to counter dominant beliefs about how people of size ought to act. As highlighted in the works of recent performance scholars, stigmatized individuals, among them people who are disabled, fat, or facing intersectional oppression like Asian-American gays, have used further performative strategies for managing stigma. Chemers explores how social deviants tackle stigma from the stage, while Han gives us the idea of using performativity as a strategy to counter the stigma of occupying two marginal identities (gay and Asian) in the United States; and LeBesco focuses on the politics of fat oppression and "performing fatness."[9] In turn, I am interested in how the big men in Girth and Mirth play up their stigma to the hilt, highlighting rather than minimizing it, thus using it to reconfigure their shame. I note how they make size a kind of performance in and of itself.

In his discussion of disability and freak shows, Chemers sees a connection between disability, other forms of stigma, and theatricality. À la Goffman, he points out that stigmatized persons are asked to perform inferiority. He argues "identity is *performative*. . . . Stigma must, at some point or other, be staged" with over-the-top antics in order for the stigmatized to gain the upper hand.[10] Chemers sees disability as "a socially constructed form of identity, a role to be played or played against."[11] That is, stigmatized persons can gain control of their situation. He asserts "a 'spoiled identity' incorporates a certain amount of [muscle] flex[ing] in relation to the discourses that seek to marginalize it."[12]

One of the marginalizing discourses Girth & Mirthers struggle with is the respectability of their citizenship. As I demonstrate in chapter 4, at one of their national annual Convergences, big men indulge in casting themselves as classy consumers of culture. However, more often than not, at their extralocal activities they are "stultifying conformity."[13] And in doing so, they use perversion to have their own say-so. They recast themselves as sexy and offer a counterdiscourse to fat's being a turnoff.

Han focuses on gay Asian men living in the United States who constitute a minority within a minority. He argues that they have to cope with multiple marginalizations: They "must learn to manage the stigma of race from the larger society, . . . of homosexuality from both the larger society and the Asian community, . . . and the stigma of race, once more, in the gay community."[14] In their attempt to reconcile this quadruple marginalization, Han asserts, gay Asian men highlight and magnify their spoiled identities rather than minimize and downplay them. In this book, I also discuss how being both fat and gay presents multiple challenges for big gay men: homophobia and fatphobia in the larger society, a fat penalty within the gay community, not to mention the sad reality of fat discrimination among big men themselves.

LeBesco's work helps me explain Girth & Mirthers' ambiguous relationship to the norm. Sociology privileges the social deviant's desire to be bodily normal as the crux of his identity. However, my research shows that most big men are not necessarily looking to normalize their bodies but are interested in expanding and playing with what qualifies as sexy, because their sexual currency in the eyes of others remains tenuous. LeBesco's work elaborating stigma, normalcy, and politics has helped me understand Girth & Mirthers better: the layeredness of the stigma they experience, their club as a normalcy group, and how we can see the political underpinnings in a group that is cast as "social."[15] According to LeBesco, fat suits used in movies, for example, parallel the traditions of drag and blackface, and she points out that Hollywood does not go beyond these traditions. She imagines "[f]at camp could be . . . a different way of performing fat . . . , which overcomes self-hatred and a culturally imposed lack of self-esteem, rather than reinscribing [shame] on the body in the way that critics feared that drag would do."[16]

I likewise conclude in this book that the defiant strategy of camp is a more appealing and constructive way to reconfigure fat stigma. While Bakhtin considers carnival to be rejuvenating and Bateson regards play as therapeutic, I see both activities as only quick fixes.[17] In the case of the Girth & Mirthers, I found that camp turns stigma around and expands the big men's coping strategies to include everyday resistance and survival. But even so, unlike the gay Asian drag queens Han discusses, campy Girth & Mirthers still do not gain much more visibility in the gay community than they previously had.

LeBesco hints that gay men do not find much refuge from sizism in queer circles. Likewise, I argue that the gay community is not going to accept and assimilate its big brethren with open arms. The problem is not that the alphabet soup of LGBT and beyond is exhausted. It is not a matter of its being unable to accommodate any more categories; rather, the issue is a resistance to size.

According to LeBesco, the National Association to Advance Fat Acceptance has experienced within-group conflict as to whether to regard fat as normal or as a disability, a change in status which would be categorized as corporeal deviance and thus a double whammy: a fat stigma and a disability stigma.[18] It is quite fascinating, therefore, that the big men minimize disability even though they are acutely aware of it, because a few of their members no longer work and are on disability. Lucy Aphramor writes: "There is a sense of recalcitrance around allowing for fatness as disability."[19] Charlotte Cooper concurs: "In size acceptance communities I sense a palpable fear of disability."[20] The question is why Girth & Mirthers would relinquish the possibility of having disability status, which might grant them a form of face-saving; however, the possibility of embarrassment remains a formidable barrier to adopting this status. Thus it makes sense that the big men in my study do not claim disability much; and if it comes up, they try to sidestep that discourse. While these same big men tiptoe less around size and sexuality, they understandably do so around physical disability, because adding it on top of being fat and gay would be triply stigmatizing. Cooper relates what the sentiment might be: "[I]mpaired is too charged a label for fat people, since it implies . . . the physical ill health, disease and low medical status from which fat people are struggling to distance [themselves]."[21]

Sometimes, the stigmatized have to act larger than life to gain exposure, rather than always remain isolated in the safety of the Girth & Mirth community they have built. When they do so, acting campy and kitschy, they challenge certain deeply held prejudices about human difference. I see big men's play as *challenging* stigma versus playing a stigmatized role. For instance, the Girth & Mirthers engage in rebellious activities unrepentantly as if to say, "You think our bodies are revolting, let us show you just how disgusting we can be," or with unbridled campiness they let it all hang out, keeping one step ahead of what people are thinking about them, so that they do not allow others the chance to say it first. In the acceptance of "stigma as *fait accompli*," this "I'll-show-you" attitude flies in the face of the activist mission.[22] The big men renegotiate the terms of their stigma, but do not necessarily battle it through public education, so to speak. Yet, there are many strands of fat activism, and not all seek to educate.

In other instances, the big men stage replacement activities such as a big men's dance, which approximates a gay prom, to gain some semblance of normalcy. In this dance of difference, they are able to perform and exercise their citizenship, albeit within a circumscribed "safe" space. Such proxy activities are "necessary whenever the general social matrix suffers a significant loss that leaves a discernible gulf between that ideal society and the disappointments of reality."[23] In this way, the replacement activity "requires the construction of elaborate systems of belief that patch over the inconsistencies, and these systems must be embodied by physical performance."[24] Judith Butler, of course, is the obvious example of a scholar who has made an entire career out of doing this kind of work on performance and embodiment, her focus being on "doing" gender.[25] It is interesting that the Girth & Mirthers do not perform gender exclusively, but also carry out ritualized performances, such as the repeated antics in which they engage every year at their reunions, and birthday or food rituals in which they engage in order to reclaim a sense of normalcy.

NOTES

NOTES TO THE INTRODUCTION

1. "Camp" is privileged tongue-in-cheek humor among insiders.
2. While there is no one correct ethical answer here, it is crucial to recognize the ethical compromises. Kirin Narayan talks about her own experience as a field-worker when she felt ethically challenged while both following and researching a Hindu teacher. The *swamiji* she was studying pointed out that Narayan was serving two masters (the *swamiji* himself and her dissertation committee) and her loyalties were divided between the two.

   Tamar El-Or faced a similar ethical dilemma when she was researching Ortho-dox Jews and the participants tried to persuade her to take a ritual bath, which she had no intention of doing. She thought it deceptive and unethical to lead them on and therefore discontinued her research. However, as I learned from another Jewish researcher studying the same community, the members believe that as long as they keep the nonpracticing Jewish researcher engaged in their lives, there is always a possibility she will be persuaded to take part in the ritual sooner or later. This example may very well suggest that researchers, in their attempt to protect participants, sometimes overlook their agency. For more on confessional tales of ethical uncertainties, see Van Maanen, *Tales of the Field*, 73–100.
3. Like its counterparts *chub* and *big man*, *chaser* will be discussed at more length in other areas of the book.
4. Brown, "Wounded Attachments."

NOTES TO CHAPTER 1

1. The early history of Girth & Mirth is murky. Nathaniel Pyle and Michael Loewy chronicle Girth & Mirth's history, based on the original created by Alex Textor in

1999. They document in a concise seven-page chapter the emergence of big men's networks showing the formation of local Girth & Mirth clubs and the formation of the national Affiliated Bigmen's Clubs.

2. See, for instance, Textor, "Organization, Specialization, and Desires in the Big Men's Movement"; Blank, *Big Big Love*, 61–62; Bunzl, "Chasers"; Hennen, "Bear Bodies, Bear Masculinity"; Hennen, *Faeries, Bears, and Leathermen*; Pyle and Loewy, "Double Stigma"; Pyle and Klein, "Fat. Hairy. Sexy."

3. Textor, "Organization, Specialization, and Desires in the Big Men's Movement." Millman notes in *Such a Pretty Face* that the National Association to Advance Fat Acceptance was founded by an average-sized man who found fat women attractive and married a fat woman. Interestingly, Girth & Mirth was also started not by a big man, but by his admirer—that is, an "outsider." In other words, sexual objectification was central to the inception of both clubs.

4. One of the men of Girth & Mirth whom I met at a Labor Day weekend reunion for big men told me, "I think the original New York Girth & Mirth was born out of NAAFA, which started in New York in the late '60s." I also learned from him that the couple who founded the club had connections with NAAFA. Though this is all speculative, it may provide a clue as to how Girth & Mirth came about: by some members of NAAFA striking out on their own. Furthermore, the timeline seems to fit—Girth & Mirth's beginnings in 1976 fall in line with NAAFA's earlier inception in 1969.

5. Textor, "Organization, Specialization, and Desires in the Big Men's Movement."

6. Pyle and Loewy, "Double Stigma."

7. McNally, *The Ritz*. This historical fact is also part of the cultural memory of members of the group.

8. It is interesting that the first popular reference to big gay men comes from a fictionalized sex-crazed chaser.

9. Textor, "Organization, Specialization, and Desires in the Big Men's Movement."

10. Textor has done a content analysis of magazines and websites to show how the big men's movement initially organized. He also accounts for how it garnered a national presence as well as a transnational one. It was not within the scope of his analysis to look at documents from local clubs. Though analyzing documents can be valuable, such documents must not be privileged over real-life experience. Therefore, there is good reason to focus on the local culture, so that we learn about real people's real experiences in real spaces. My book is ethnographic rather than a historical account or a content analysis of magazines and websites. It is based on data from participant observation and interviews, wherein I focus on lived experience and human interactions.

11. The Girth & Mirthers do not necessarily obsess about dieting, though some moderate their use of sugar. For example, I was not given any specific instructions for what to bring to the first pot-luck I attended, other than "We are not diet-fussy too much, but the beverages are usually sugar-free."

12. The phrase "you don't have to apologize for your size" comes from the subtitle to Marilyn Wann's classic book on size acceptance. See Wann, *Fat!So?*

13. For instance, the kaffeeklatsch I describe in the Introduction offers a time and place for a kind of intimacy wherein big men come together to socialize around coffee and cheesecake.

14. At the same time, even when they go out to eat as a group, there is the risk of their being perceived by the fatphobic public as looking like a "herd," thus attracting attention and still being separated from the larger society.

15. Millman, *Such a Pretty Face.*

16. Smith, *Lectures on the Religion of Semites*, 247 (as cited in Mennell et al., *The Sociology of Food*, 115).

17. Van Gennep, *The Rites of Passage*, 29 (as cited in Mennell et al., *The Sociology of Food*, 115).

18. With regard to the reference to Paula Deen's banana pudding, well before Deen's 2013 fall from grace for her racist remarks, Girth & Mirthers' celebration of food is melded with pop culture, all in the spirit of play or corniness. The southern chef had become a novelty for big gay men; she had a gay assistant and had in fact spoken out against gay bullying. She has been fat herself, and in the media she has often been scolded for making people fat.

19. Here, the term *intimacy* refers less to sexuality and more to commensality, or what Michael Herzfeld describes as the "cultural intimacies" of groups with a "rueful self-recognition" that they are a public embarrassment to others. Herzfeld, *Cultural Intimacy*, 6.

20. Simmel, "Sociology of the Meal."

21. Pyle and Loewy, "Double Stigma."

22. Martin, "Organizational Approaches to Shame," 125–26.

23. Britt and Heise, "From Shame to Pride in Identity Politics."

24. Hanisch, "The Personal Is Political."

25. It is ironic that the one area in which the Girth & Mirthers claim to be political is in "advancing the cause of the gay community," the very same community that rejects them. Similarly, the charity work they do for a local LGBT youth organization is also perhaps doing work for a group of people who would most likely not sign on to their cause.

26. This would have been akin to mistaking Girth & Mirthers for a more radical group like the Rad Fatties—radical female fat activists.

27. Monaghan, "Big Handsome Men, Bears and Others."

28. Millman, *Such a Pretty Face.*

29. See Saguy and Ward, "Coming Out as Fat."

30. Goffman, *Stigma*, 103. If fat people "fail" to adopt what Goffman calls "the right line"—going on fad diets, exercising, and so on—they are not granted full citizenship; and if they ask for citizenship without making an effort to "conform," they are seen as disrupting the social order. Furthermore, because fat has become

pathologized as the "disease" of obesity and this "disease" is thought to be curable, there is tacit consent that they must normalize their bodies to thin ones if they wish to become eligible to participate fully in society.

31. Chemers, *Staging Stigma*, 20.
32. The Chub-and-Chaser Contest and sexualizing around the pool are described in detail in chapters 3 and 4.
33. On the whole, Girth & Mirthers' efforts are not made toward achieving "acceptable" bodies; nor are they intended toward legitimizing obesity. Out of hundreds of big men I met both locally and extralocally, I encountered only four who had opted for bariatric surgery; and I can recall only one memorable case that stands out, that of a local big man who tried various fad diets and exercise regimens and felt repeatedly defeated by his multiple attempts. Usually, rather than buy into body modification packages, which include plastic surgery, bariatric surgery, or liposuction, big men mostly want to have a sense of normalcy and citizenship. I also met a few men in the group who identified with the spirit of shows like *The Biggest Loser*. It was in fact difficult to get many of my friends, some of whom are fellow gays and lesbians, to understand why I would deem these supposed "losers" worthy of research. Yet it was precisely *because* of these contradictions that I persisted with this project.

NOTES TO CHAPTER 2

1. *Skinny and Fatty*, directed by N. Terao.
2. Monaghan, "Civilising Recalcitrant Boys' Bodies."
3. Probyn, "Everyday Shame." Note that some fat studies scholars take serious issue with Probyn's later article "Silences Behind the Mantra: Critiquing Feminist Fat." See Kirkland, "The Environmental Account of Obesity"; Cooper, "Fat Studies."
4. Goffman, *Stigma*.
5. Whitesel, "Gay Men's Use of Online Pictures in Fat-Affirming Groups"; Whitesel, "Fatvertising."
6. LeBesco, "Revolting Bodies."
7. Monaghan, *Men and the War on Obesity*.
8. *Pretty Woman*, directed by Garry Marshall.
9. Goffman, *Behavior in Public Places*, 83.
10. Goffman, *Stigma*; Goode, "The Stigma of Obesity"; Goode, "Physical Characteristics as Deviance." It is important to note that the cited author, Erich Goode, later admitted in his confessional article "Sexual Involvement and Social Research in a Fat Civil Rights Organization" to exploitation of his research subjects. See the Winter 2002 issue of *Qualitative Sociology*; an entire edition of the journal was dedicated to critiquing Goode's researcher ethics.
11. Moi, "Appropriating Bourdieu," 1018.
12. Durkheim, *The Rules of the Sociological Method*.
13. Bourdieu, *Masculine Domination*, 1.

14. This Girth & Mirther's being given an unnecessary battery of tests would be akin to women's being sold needless hysterectomies. See Diana Scully, "Negotiating to Do Surgery."

15. For example, a previous study shows that women's coronary concerns were taken less seriously by male medical staff than those of men, because women were reduced to whiners, so they were at a more advanced stage of heart disease by the time they were treated. Profiling women in this manner delayed their treatment and rendered them two times more likely to die during bypass surgery. See Jerry Bishop, "Study Finds Doctors Tend to Postpone Heart Surgery for Women, Raising Risk."

16. William and Dorothy Thomas, *The Child in America*, 572.

17. Researchers are finding that heterosexual men are less and less exempt from body image concerns. For them, these concerns fluctuate depending on age, stage in the life course, relationship status, or belonging to a sports team (e.g., bodybuilders who identify as heterosexual).

18. Millman, *Such a Pretty Face*, 244–45.

19. Body aesthetics are culture-bound, and here I am referring to those produced by Western consumer culture.

20. Blotcher, "Justify My Love Handles"; Drummond, "Men's Bodies"; Padva, "Heavenly Monsters."

21. Jennifer Taub found that bisexual women reported being more comfortable with their bodies when they were involved with women than with men. See Taub, "Bisexual Women and Beauty Norms." Transgender author S. Bear Bergman describes experiencing size differently depending on whether onlookers perceive Bear as a woman or as a man. See Bergman, "Part-Time Fatso."

22. Millman, *Such a Pretty Face*.

23. Goffman, *Stigma*, 30–31.

24. See Millman, *Such a Pretty Face*, for an elaboration of this concept of the "bad boy" flaunting the limits of his bad behavior in front of his fat mommy—in this case, fat daddy.

25. Ibid., 168.

26. Prohaska and Gailey's research into "hogging" is regarded to be the definitive work on this subject. See Prohaska and Gailey, "Achieving Masculinity through Sexual Predation"; Gailey and Prohaska, "'Knocking off a Fat Girl'"; Prohaska and Gailey, "Fat Women as 'Easy Targets.'"

27. Millman, *Such a Pretty Face*.

28. Kimmel, *Guyland*.

29. Giles, "A Matter of Size."

30. Goode, "Physical Characteristics as Deviance," 328.

31. Bell and McNaughton, "Feminism and the Invisible Fat Man"; Durgadas, "Fatness and the Feminized Man." An anonymous reviewer of this growing line of research into fat's being demoted as a subordinated masculinity suggested that when

thinking in terms of sustaining a normatively masculine identity, feminization can be disruptive in ways personally damaging to some men. However, this as a social construct is damaging to women also—being seen as more like a woman might not be the worst thing in the world. While this is clearly an important element of fat masculinity, continued research into these claims is required, at the very least because it challenges the stability of polarized gender norms upheld by such observations.

32. Millman, *Such a Pretty Face.*
33. Bergling, *Sissyphobia*; Connell, "A Very Straight Gay."
34. Millman, *Such a Pretty Face.*
35. To protect the identity of the participants, all names have been changed.
36. Millman, *Such a Pretty Face*, 245.
37. Probyn, "Everyday Shame," 328.
38. Britt and Heise, "From Shame to Pride in Identity Politics."
39. Hennen, *Faeries, Bears, and Leathermen.*
40. Goffman, *The Presentation of Self in Everyday Life.*
41. Ibid.

NOTES TO CHAPTER 3

1. The name of this motel is fictionalized yet intentionally similar to the original. I adhere to Peter Elbow's argument in his book *Writing with Power*, in which he talks about writing authentically and upholding a magical view of language. Elbow boils it down as follows: a "word is a part of the thing it stands for—the word contains some of the juice or essence or soul of the thing it points to" (358). So, in the spirit of Elbow, even though I changed the name of the motel for anonymity, I still chose a pseudonym close in sound in order to keep the flair of the original resort name. I respect the privacy and anonymity of the people I studied. In some cases when I anonymized names, I tried to remain loyal to the essence and spirit the real name seemed to convey. In other cases, the names of places and nicknames of people were so fitting that I left them alone. Finally, I also intentionally retained essential biographical facts about people, while altering less significant markers of identity in an effort to anonymize the data. In the end, I trust I did not give away anyone's secrets, while still doing justice to the spirit of each person and setting. Finally, I would like to directly address readers who might recognize themselves as having participated in the event: I apologize in advance if I have misrepresented or offended anyone in any way.
2. Goffman, "Supportive Interchanges," 73.
3. Bakhtin, *Rabelais and His World*, 10.
4. Ibid., 166.
5. Wann, *Fat!So?*, 168.
6. Rogers, "Big Girls, Don't Cry."

7. Balcony bingo is reminiscent of carnival behavior that has its roots in gambling and in street fairs.
8. Bakhtin, "Characteristics of Genre and Plot Comparison in Dostoevsky's Works," 122.
9. Sontag, "Notes on 'Camp,'" 63.
10. The nickname B.J., short for "blowjob," was given to him over the weekend.
11. In Bear culture, it is customary to "woof" at a sexy guy.
12. Bakhtin, "Characteristics of Genre and Plot Comparison in Dostoevsky's Works," 123.
13. Ibid., 128.
14. While fat activists are against gastric bypass surgery, the Girth & Mirth organization has not made any official statement on the topic. But locally, most Girth & Mirthers I interviewed said they were personally opposed to the surgery, at the same time believing that people should have the freedom to make their own choices. One club member said the club has no official position on dieting, gastric bypass surgery, or plastic surgery. While he was personally opposed to liposuction, and he would never do gastric bypass, he felt that people have the right to make their own decisions. Another big man said that surgery is invasive, expensive, and vain, though he does not think there is any consensus among club members on topics like weight loss, gastric surgery, and dieting. One big man shared his experience with a doctor who was pushing for gastric bypass, which he resisted. First, he did not want to have a scar. Second, as a nurse he had witnessed people experiencing complications with these surgeries and even dying. While he would not deny others' having this surgery, he would not choose it for himself. One Girth & Mirther remarked that gastric bypass is dangerous, though he would not take issue with other people's choices, particularly when it may be their only choice. Yet another Girth & Mirther said he struggles with his weight every single day, and he can see why people turn to surgery. Finally, one big man I interviewed had gastric bypass upon his doctor's warning that he could die if he did not reduce his weight. He said at first he was too big to have the surgery without its posing a threat to his life. He therefore lost weight in order to have the surgery. Though in the aftermath he finds some foods hard to eat without becoming sick, he is still pleased with the results enough to say, "I'd do it again in a heartbeat." Overall, though Girth & Mirth has no formal position on these gastric surgeries, there seems to be an informal position to respect others' freedom of choice.
15. Throughout my analysis of this weekend, I have grappled with my somewhat covert researcher position. I did not want to interfere by prefacing every encounter with an announcement that I was a researcher and not a "real" guest at the event. Some readers may interpret my choice to keep quiet as usurping the agency of the participants. To the contrary, my depiction of being propositioned in the pool shows clearly that my suitor indeed had agency. My response was truthful

when I said I was unavailable; I simply did not volunteer that I was there to research, not play. Another example of this agency is my key informants' recruiting me to their own purposes by giving me the job of filling in for a coordinator who had canceled at the last minute.

16. Cleto, *Camp*, 8.
17. Wann, *Fat!So?*, 168.
18. Bakhtin, *Rabelais and His World*, 10.
19. In fact, in Ohio when the organizers were planning for the Super Weekend show, one of the men got off track and said, "We wanted Janet Jackson for the halftime, but couldn't get her to come for some tit-flashing." Then, he and another planner across the room lifted up their shirts and showed us their "man boobs." In essence, the events of the whole weekend are one big "planned" malfunction.
20. The motel's shutting down the glory hole window was another instance of censoring.
21. Bakhtin, *Rabelais and His World*, 19.
22. Bakhtin, "Characteristics of Genre and Plot Comparison in Dostoevsky's Works," 133.
23. Goffman, *Stigma*.
24. Steinem (1981), as cited in Wann, "Taking the Waters," 41.
25. Ibid.
26. Ibid.
27. Wann, "Taking the Waters," 41.
28. Goffman, *Asylums*.
29. Easto and Truzzi, "Towards an Ethnography of the Carnival Social System," 550.
30. Babcock, *The Reversible World*, 24.
31. Cleto, *Camp*, 8.
32. Sontag, "Notes on 'Camp,'" 59.
33. Cleto, *Camp*, 8.
34. Bateson, *Steps to an Ecology of Mind*, 139. Likewise, sociologist George Herbert Mead thought play was critical to self-development. See Mead, "Play, the Game, and the Generalized Other."
35. Bateson also argues that play can take the ritual forms of hazing or kidding, which I had experienced in the pool, when the big men heckled me about my being a sunburned twink when they tried to initiate me into the weekend.
36. Goffman, *Stigma*, 53.
37. Although big men's response to shame is to play with it, my data leads me to make an alternative reading of the weekend. Ann Swidler, in her book *Talk of Love*, suggests that organizational intimacy, as exemplified in big gay men's sheltering, represents "strategies of action." Rather than socially isolate themselves with their shame, the big men create an environment that fosters intimate friendship, a strategy of action that would indeed be political.

38. Babcock, *The Reversible World*, 14.
39. Ibid., 22.
40. Ibid., 28.
41. Ibid., 32.

NOTES TO CHAPTER 4

1. Babcock, *The Reversible World*; Bakhtin, *Rabelais and His World*; Turner, *Dramas, Fields, and Metaphors*.
2. Pyle and Loewy, "Double Stigma."
3. Ibid.
4. In his work *Distinction*, Bourdieu asserts that a tight coupling exists between social class and aesthetic taste. A group's taste signals social distinction. That is, "good taste" can confer a sense of cultural superiority.
5. Ibid., 163–64.
6. Bourdieu, *Distinction*.
7. Ibid., 378.
8. Bourdieu, *Distinction*.
9. Noyes, *Fire in the Placa*.
10. Goffman, *Stigma*, 30–31.
11. Millman, *Such a Pretty Face*.
12. Madonna, "Justify My Love."
13. Goffman, *The Presentation of Self in Everyday Life*, 83.
14. Prohaska and Gailey, "Achieving Masculinity through Sexual Predation"; Gailey and Prohaska, "'Knocking off a Fat Girl'"; Prohaska and Gailey, "Fat Women as 'Easy Targets.'"
15. Gardner, *Passing By*.
16. Millman, *Such a Pretty Face*, 191.
17. k.d. lang, "Big-Boned Gal."
18. Bourdieu, *Distinction*, 2.
19. Bourdieu, *Distinction*.
20. Then again, there actually are gay proms or big fat queer proms for women.
21. Bourdieu, *Distinction*. Queer approaches to this conservatism would have to read against the grain to see how the big men want to have it both ways. They appropriate many of the signifying systems of heterosexual cultural practices, the very practices they have been excluded from, and resignify them. At the extralocal weekend events, the big men perform for and among themselves for the most part, though there are examples of Girth & Mirthers in Gay Pride parades where they perform for other-sized gay men, as well. At all of these events, they do not try to be acceptable to straight culture, but instead use some of the same mechanisms Bourdieu describes for their insider culture.
22. My qualitative data does not allow me to quantify how widespread is the sentiment of this one Girth & Mirther that there is an inverse relationship between

social class and masculinity. That is, as social class increases, masculinity decreases. It is impossible to extrapolate from the one quotation I provide.

23. This topic of gaining/encouraging is beyond the scope of my analysis in this book, given that most Girth & Mirthers do not support this behavior.

24. Coincidentally, his partner with whom he was writing a scholarly paper on the chub/chaser subculture was a graduate student studying with one of my past professors. His partner self-identifies as a chaser and has been a member of both the big men's and Bear communities since the late 1990s. See Pyle and Klein, "Fat. Hairy. Sexy," 81. As academic insiders and part of a collaborating couple, they have published their paper as a chapter in an edited book. See Pyle and Loewy, "Double Stigma."

25. For more on multicultural capital, see Weininger, "Pierre Bourdieu on Social Class and Symbolic Violence."

26. Veblen, *The Theory of the Leisure Class.*

27. Bourdieu, *Distinction.*

NOTES TO CHAPTER 5

1. "Water sports/golden showers" refers to being sexually aroused by urinating on someone or being urinated on. This is clinically called "urophilia."

2. Moon and Sedgwick, "Divinity."

3. Ibid., 230.

4. Britt and Heise, "From Shame to Pride in Identity Politics," 254.

5. Ibid.

6. Connolly (1999) as cited in Probyn, "Everyday Shame," 346.

7. Sedgwick, "Shame, Theatricality, and Queer Performativity," 64–65.

8. I have noticed that the Bears have recently started to organize their own special events during Gay Days in Orlando.

9. Sykes and Matza, "Techniques of Neutralization," 668. See also Scott and Lyman, "Accounts," 51; and Monaghan, *Men and the War on Obesity: A Sociological Study,* 73–116.

10. Halberstam, "Shame and White Gay Masculinity," 233.

11. Simply put, body talk is engaging in petty remarks about others' bodies. Katherine Young writes about the multiple conditions in which folks do or do not engage in body talk. See the Preface and Introduction to Young's edited book *Bodylore.*

12. Van Iquity, "Drags on Parade."

13. Probyn, "Everyday Shame," 329.

14. Walters, *All the Rage.*

15. Goffman, *Stigma,* 103.

16. Ibid.

17. LeBesco, *Revolting Bodies?*

18. Ibid., 72.

19. LeBesco, *Revolting Bodies?*

20. Ibid. An example of fat protest in pop culture is the recent stunt by the *Parks and Recreation* actor Jim O'Heir, a big man, that was filmed for a late-night talk show with host Jimmy Kimmel. O'Heir went into Abercrombie & Fitch, which refuses to stock plus sizes and prides itself in selling only to "good-looking" people. He said he was buying three shirts for someone else. After he purchased the shirts, he laid them out on a bench outside the store and cut each of them lengthwise, then reassembled them to make one plus-sized shirt using fabric tape and a stapler, with butterfly clips on the back to hold it all together. He then put the garment on and skipped merrily down the sidewalk. The clip of his stunt can be found on YouTube and elsewhere on the Internet.
21. Martin, "Organizational Approaches to Shame."
22. Halberstam, "Shame and White Gay Masculinity," 229.
23. Britt and Heise, "From Shame to Pride in Identity Politics," 256–57.
24. LeBesco, *Revolting Bodies?*
25. Butler, *Undoing Gender.*
26. Sedgwick, "Shame, Theatricality, and Queer Performativity," 64.
27. Halberstam, "Shame and White Gay Masculinity," 229.
28. Bersani, "Is the Rectum a Grave?", 208.
29. Sedgwick, "Shame and Performativity."
30. Ibid., 210–11.
31. Scheff, *Microsociology.*
32. Ibid., 172. The above speaker's campy remark does not claim to be P.C.; it is *intentionally* in poor taste. Clearly, the speaker's purely playful remark about his roommate's ample body getting squeezed into a corset is both a parody of the scene from *Gone with the Wind* and crass humor that does not censor the film's racist undertones.
33. The Bearilyn Birthday Wish was indeed video-recorded and later posted online.
34. Ben-Itzak, "I Am Not 'Explicit.'"
35. "Capping" refers to playfully insulting someone.
36. A nickname used for an effeminate gay man.
37. In thinking about fighting abjection, see Deborah McPhail, who builds on the works of Julia Kristeva and Judith Butler. As McPhail states, "[T]he abject is, in the end, an integral part of the Self through and against which the subject is defined" (1024).
38. Samantha Murray explains that even as she tried to embrace fat activism as it was prescribed by Wann, she felt ambiguous about "living [her] fat body." She writes, "[T]he ways in which I live my fat body are always multiple, contradictory, and eminently ambiguous" (270).

NOTES TO THE CONCLUSION
1. To be fair, it is not so easy to be a chaser either, as chasers are looked down upon for their choice of sex object.

2. On the flip side, all activist groups unwittingly exclude some group(s) and have to be held accountable, as was the case in the HRC example.

NOTE TO THE METHODOLOGICAL APPENDIX
1. Textor, "Organization, Specialization, and Desires in the Big Men's Movement"; Bunzl, "Chasers"; Hennen, "Bear Bodies, Bear Masculinity."

NOTES TO THE THEORETICAL APPENDIX
1. Goffman, *Stigma*, 13.
2. Scambler, "Health-related Stigma."
3. Thomas, "Theorising Disability and Chronic Illness," 215.
4. Scambler, "Health-related Stigma," 442.
5. Durkheim, *The Rules of the Sociological Method.*
6. Ibid., 445, 450.
7. Thomas, "Theorising Disability and Chronic Illness," 213.
8. LeBesco, *Revolting Bodies?* 95.
9. Chemers, *Staging Stigma*; Han, "Asian Girls Are Prettier"; LeBesco, "Situating Fat Suits," 231.
10. Chemers, *Staging Stigma*, 23.
11. Ibid.
12. Ibid.
13. Chemers, *Staging Stigma*, 4.
14. Han, "Asian Girls Are Prettier," 107.
15. LeBesco, *Revolting Bodies?*
16. LeBesco, "Situating Fat Suits," 233.
17. Bakhtin, *Rabelais and His World*; Bateson, *Steps to an Ecology of Mind.*
18. LeBesco, *Revolting Bodies?*
19. Aphramor, "Disability and the Anti-Obesity Offensive," 903.
20. Cooper, "Can a Fat Woman Call Herself Disabled," 34.
21. Ibid., 39.
22. Chemers, *Staging Stigma*, 17.
23. Ibid., 18.
24. Ibid.
25. Butler, *Undoing Gender.*

REFERENCES

Aphramor, Lucy. "Disability and the Anti-Obesity Offensive." *Disability & Society* 24, no. 7 (December 2009): 897–909.

Babcock, Barbara. *The Reversible World: Symbolic Inversion in Art and Society.* Ithaca, N.Y.: Cornell University Press, 1978.

Bakhtin, Mikhail. "Characteristics of Genre and Plot Comparison in Dostoevsky's Works." In *Problems of Dostoevsky's Poetics*, 1929/1963, edited and translated by Caryl Emerson, 101–80. Minneapolis: University of Minnesota Press, 1984.

———. *Rabelais and His World*, 1965, translated by Helene Iswolsky. Cambridge, Mass.: MIT Press, 1968.

Bateson, Gregory. *Steps to an Ecology of Mind: Collected Essays in Anthropology, Psychiatry, Evolution, and Epistemology.* Chicago: University of Chicago Press, 1972.

Bell, Kirsten, and Darlene McNaughton. "Feminism and the Invisible Fat Man." *Body & Society* 13, no. 1 (March 2007): 107–31.

Ben-Itzak, Paul. "I Am Not 'Explicit': All the Nudes Too Fat to Print." *The Dance Insider*, May 15, 2007, http://www.danceinsider.com/chevalier.html. Paid access fee.

Bergling, Tim. *Sissyphobia: Gay Men and Effeminate Behavior.* New York: Haworth Press, 2001.

Bergman, S. Bear. "Part-Time Fatso." In *The Fat Studies Reader*, edited by Esther Rothblum and Sondra Solovay, 139–42. New York: New York University Press, 2009.

Bersani, Leo. "Is the Rectum a Grave?" In *AIDS: Cultural Analysis/Cultural Activism*, edited by Douglas Crimp, 197–222. Cambridge, Mass.: MIT Press, 1987.

Bishop, Jerry. "Study Finds Doctors Tend to Postpone Heart Surgery for Women, Raising Risk." *Wall Street Journal* (April 16, 1990): B4.

Blank, Hanne. *Big Big Love, Revised: A Sex and Relationships Guide for People of Size (and Those Who Love Them)*. New York: Celestial Arts/Random House, 2011.

Blotcher, Jay. "Justify My Love Handles: How the Queer Community Trims the Fat." In *Looking Queer: Body Image and Identity in Lesbian, Bisexual, Gay, and Transgender Communities*, edited by Dawn Atkins, 359–66. New York: Harrington Park Press, 1998.

Bourdieu, Pierre. *Distinction: A Social Critique of the Judgement of Taste*, 1979, translated by Richard Nice. Cambridge, Mass.: Harvard University Press, 1984.

———. *Masculine Domination*. Stanford, Calif.: Stanford University Press, 2001.

Britt, Lory, and David Heise. "From Shame to Pride in Identity Politics." In *Self, Identity, and Social Movements*, edited by Sheldon Stryker, Timothy Owens, and Robert White, 252–68. Minneapolis: University of Minnesota Press, 2000.

Brown, Wendy. "Wounded Attachments." *Political Theory* 21, no. 3 (August 1993): 390–410.

Bunzl, Matti. "Chasers." In *Fat: The Anthropology of an Obsession*, edited by Don Kulick and Anne Meneley, 199–210. New York: Penguin, 2005.

Butler, Judith. *Undoing Gender*. New York: Routledge, 2004.

Chemers, Michael. *Staging Stigma: A Critical Examination of the American Freak Show*. New York: Palgrave Macmillan, 2008.

Cleto, Fabio, ed. *Camp: Queer Aesthetics and the Performing Subject: A Reader*. Ann Arbor: University of Michigan Press, 2002.

Connell, Raewyn. "A Very Straight Gay: Masculinity, Homosexual Experience, and the Dynamics of Gender." *American Sociological Review* 57, no. 6 (December 1992): 735–51.

Cooper, Charlotte. "Can a Fat Woman Call Herself Disabled?" *Disability & Society* 12, no. 1 (February 1997): 31–41.

———. "Fat Studies: Mapping the Field." *Sociology Compass* 4, no. 12 (December 2010): 1020–34.

Drummond, Murray. "Men's Bodies: Listening to the Voices of Young Gay Men." *Men and Masculinities* 7, no. 3 (January 2005): 270–90.

Durgadas, Ganapati. "Fatness and the Feminized Man." In *Looking Queer: Body Image and Identity in Lesbian, Bisexual, Gay, and Transgender Communities*, edited by Dawn Atkins, 367–71. New York: Harrington Park Press, 1998.

Durkheim, Emile. *The Rules of the Sociological Method and Selected Texts on Sociology and Its Method*, 1895, edited by Steven Lukes, translated by Wilfred Halls. New York: Free Press/Macmillan, 1982.

Easto, Patrick, and Marcello Truzzi. "Towards an Ethnography of the Carnival Social System." *The Journal of Popular Culture* 6, no. 3 (Spring 1973): 550–66.

Elbow, Peter. "Writing and Magic." In *Writing with Power: Techniques for Mastering the Writing Process*, 357–74. New York: Oxford University Press, 1981.

El-Or, Tamar. "Do You Really Know How They Make Love? The Limits on Intimacy with Ethnographic Informants." *Qualitative Sociology* 15, no. 1 (Spring 1992): 53–72.

Farrell, Amy. *Fat Shame: Stigma and the Fat Body in American Culture*. New York: New York University Press, 2011.

Gailey, Jeannine, and Ariane Prohaska. "'Knocking Off a Fat Girl': An Exploration of Hogging, Male Sexuality and Neutralizations." *Deviant Behavior* 27, no. 1 (February 2006): 31–49.

Gardner, Carol. *Passing By: Gender and Public Harassment*. Berkeley and Los Angeles: University of California Press, 1995.

Giles, Patrick. "A Matter of Size." In *Looking Queer: Body Image and Identity in Lesbian, Bisexual, Gay, and Transgender Communities*, edited by Dawn Atkins, 355–57. New York: Harrington Park Press, 1998.

Goffman, Erving. *The Presentation of Self in Everyday Life*. New York: Anchor Books/Doubleday, 1959.

———. *Asylums: Essays on the Social Situation of Mental Patients and Other Inmates*. Garden City, N.Y.: Anchor Books/Doubleday, 1961.

———. *Behavior in Public Places: Notes on the Social Organization of Gatherings*. New York: Free Press, 1963.

———. *Stigma: Notes on the Management of Spoiled Identity*. Englewood Cliffs, N.J.: Prentice-Hall, 1963.

———. "Supportive Interchanges." In *Relations in Public: Microstudies of the Public Order*, 62–94. New York: Basic Books, 1971.

Goode, Erich. "Sexual Involvement and Social Research in a Fat Civil Rights Organization." *Qualitative Sociology* 25, no. 4 (Winter 2002): 501–34.

———. "The Stigma of Obesity." In *Readings in Deviant Behavior*, edited by Alex Thio and Thomas C. Calhoun, 176–82. Boston: Pearson/Allyn & Bacon, 2004.

———. "Physical Characteristics as Deviance." In *Deviant Behavior*, 324–51. Upper Saddle River, N.J.: Pearson Education, 2005.

Halberstam, Judith (Jack). "Shame and White Gay Masculinity." *Social Text* 23, no. 84–85 (Fall–Winter 2005): 219–33.

Han, Chong-Suk. "Asian Girls Are Prettier: Gendered Presentations as Stigma Management among Gay Asian Men." *Symbolic Interaction* 32, no. 2 (Spring 2009): 106–22.

Hanisch, Carol. "The Personal Is Political" [1969]. In *Notes from the Second Year: Women's Liberation: Major Writings of the Radical Feminists*, edited by Shulamith Firestone and Anne Koedt, 76–77. New York: Radical Feminism, 1970.

Hennen, Peter. "Bear Bodies, Bear Masculinity: Recuperation, Resistance, or Retreat?" *Gender & Society* 19, no. 1 (February 2005): 25–43.

———. *Faeries, Bears, and Leathermen: Men in Community Queering the Masculine*. Chicago: University of Chicago Press, 2008.

Herzfeld, Michael. *Cultural Intimacy: Social Poetics in the Nation-State*. New York: Routledge, 2005.

Kimmel, Michael. *Guyland: The Perilous World Where Boys Become Men*. New York: HarperCollins, 2008.

Kirkland, Anna. "The Environmental Account of Obesity: A Case for Feminist Skepticism." *Signs: Journal of Women in Culture and Society* 36, no. 2 (Winter 2011): 411–36.

lang, k.d., and the Reclines. "Big-Boned Gal," written by k.d. lang and Ben Mink. Sire Records, Album, 1989.

LeBesco, Kathleen. *Revolting Bodies? The Struggle to Redefine Fat Identity*. Amherst: University of Massachusetts Press, 2004.

———. "Situating Fat Suits: Blackface, Drag, and the Politics of Performance." *Women & Performance: A Journal of Feminist Theory* 15, no. 2 (June 2005): 231–42.

Madonna. "Justify My Love," written by Lenny Kravitz and Ingrid Chavez, with additional lyrics by Madonna, Sire Records, Compact Disc, 1990.

Martin. Daniel. "Organizational Approaches to Shame: Avowal, Management, and Contestation." *Sociological Quarterly* 41, no. 1 (Winter 2000): 125–50.

McNally, Terrence. *The Ritz*. Garden City, N.Y.: Doubleday, 1975.

McPhail, Deborah. "What to Do with the 'Tubby Hubby'? 'Obesity,' the Crisis of Masculinity, and the Nuclear Family in Early Cold War Canada." *Antipode* 41, no. 5 (November 2009): 1021–50.

Mead, George. "Play, the Game, and the Generalized Other," Section 20 in *Mind Self and Society from the Standpoint of a Social Behaviorist*, edited by Charles Morris, 152–64. Chicago: University of Chicago Press, 1934.

Mennell, Stephen, Anne Murcott, and Anneke van Otterloo. *The Sociology of Food: Eating, Diet, and Culture*. Newbury Park, Calif.: Sage Publications, 1992.

Millman, Marcia. *Such a Pretty Face: Being Fat in America*. New York: Norton, 1980.

Moi, Toril. "Appropriating Bourdieu: Feminist Theory and Pierre Bourdieu's Sociology of Culture." *New Literary History* 22, no. 4 (Autumn 1991): 1017–49.

Monaghan, Lee. "Big Handsome Men, Bears and Others: Virtual Constructions of 'Fat Male Embodiment.'" *Body & Society* 11, no. 2 (June 2005): 81–111.

———. *Men and the War on Obesity: A Sociological Study*. New York: Routledge, 2008.

———. "Civilising Recalcitrant Boys' Bodies: Pursuing Social Fitness through the Anti-Obesity Offensive." *Sport, Education, and Society*, advance online publication (August 2012), digital object identifier: 10.1080/13573322.2012.716034

Moon, Michael, and Eve Sedgwick. "Divinity: A Dossier, a Performance Piece, a Little Understood Emotion." In *Tendencies*, by Eve Sedgwick, 215–51. Durham, N.C.: Duke University Press, 1993.

Murray, Samantha. "Doing Politics or Selling Out? Living the Fat Body." *Women's Studies* 34, no. 3–4 (April 2005): 265–77.

Narayan, Kirin. *Storytellers, Saints, and Scoundrels: Folk Narrative in Hindu Religious Teaching*. Philadelphia: University of Pennsylvania Press, 1989.

Noyes, Dorothy. *Fire in the Placa: Catalan Festival Politics after Franco*. Philadelphia: University of Pennsylvania Press, 2003.

Padva, Gilad. "Heavenly Monsters: Politics of the Male Body in the Naked Issue of *Attitude* Magazine." *International Journal of Sexuality and Gender Studies* 7, no. 4 (October 2002): 281–92.

Pretty Woman, directed by Garry Marshall; written by J. F. Lawton (Theatrical release: March 23, 1990 by Touchstone Pictures).

Probyn, Elspeth. "Everyday Shame." *Cultural Studies* 18, no. 2–3 (June 2004): 329–49.

———. "Silences behind the Mantra: Critiquing Feminist Fat." *Feminism Psychology* 18, no. 3 (August 2008): 401–4.

Prohaska, Ariane, and Jeannine A. Gailey. "Fat Women as 'Easy Targets': Achieving Masculinity through Hogging." In *The Fat Studies Reader*, edited by Esther Rothblum and Sondra Solovay, 158–66. New York: New York University Press, 2009.

———. "Achieving Masculinity through Sexual Predation: The Case of Hogging." *Journal of Gender Studies* 19, no. 1 (March 2010): 13–25.

Pyle, Nathaniel, and Noa Klein. "Fat. Hairy. Sexy: Contesting Standards of Beauty and Sexuality in the Gay Community." In *Embodied Resistance: Challenging the Norms, Breaking the Rules*, edited by Chris Bobel and Samantha Kwan, 78–87. Nashville: Vanderbilt University Press, 2011.

Pyle, Nathaniel, and Michael Loewy. "Double Stigma: Fat Men and Their Male Admirers." In *The Fat Studies Reader*, edited by Esther Rothblum and Sondra Solovay, 143–50. New York: New York University Press, 2009.

Rogers, Thomas. "Big Girls, Don't Cry: The Fight for the Right to Be Fat, Queer, and Proud." *Village Voice*, June 12, 2007, http://www.villagevoice.com/2007-06-12/nyc-life/big-girls-don-t-cry/full/. Accessed July 6, 2012.

Saguy, Abigail, and Anna Ward. "Coming Out as Fat: Rethinking Stigma." *Social Psychology Quarterly* 74, no. 1 (March 2011): 53–75.

Scambler, Graham. "Health-related Stigma." *Sociology of Health & Illness* 31, no. 3 (April 2009): 441–55.

Scheff, Thomas. *Microsociology: Discourse, Emotion, and Social Structure*. Chicago: University of Chicago Press, 1994.

Scott, Marvin, and Stanford Lyman. "Accounts." *American Sociological Review* 33, no. 1 (February 1968): 46–62.

Scully, Diana. "Negotiating to Do Surgery." In *Dominant Issues in Medical Sociology*, edited by Howard Schwartz, 146–52. New York: McGraw-Hill, 1994.

Sedgwick, Eve. "Shame and Performativity: Henry James's New York Edition Prefaces." In *Henry James's New York Edition: The Construction of Authorship*, edited by David McWhirter, 206–39. Stanford, Calif.: Stanford University Press, 1995.

———. "Shame, Theatricality, and Queer Performativity: Henry James's *The Art of the Novel*." In *Touching Feeling: Affect, Pedagogy, Performativity*, by Eve Sedgwick, 35–65. Durham, N.C.: Duke University Press, 2003.

Simmel, Georg. "Sociology of the Meal," 1910. In *Simmel on Culture: Selected Writings*, edited by David Frisby and Mike Featherstone, 130–35. Thousand Oaks, Calif.: Sage Publications, 1997.

Skinny and Fatty (Chibideka Monogatari), directed by N. Terao; written by Mitsuo Wakasugi and Seiya Yoshida, *CBS Children's Film Festival with Kukla, Fran and Ollie* (Theatrical release: 1959, Japan; Episode airdate: 1965, U.S.; VHS release: 2001, by Kid Start Entertainment).

Sontag, Susan. "'Notes on 'Camp,'" 1964. In *Camp: Queer Aesthetics and the Performing Subject—A Reader*, edited by Fabio Cleto, 53–65. Ann Arbor: University of Michigan Press, 1999.

Swidler, Ann. *Talk of Love: How Culture Matters*. Chicago: University of Chicago Press, 2001.

Sykes, Gresham, and David Matza. "Techniques of Neutralization: A Theory of Delinquency." *American Sociological Review* 22, no. 6 (1957): 664–70.

Taub, Jennifer. "Bisexual Women and Beauty Norms: A Qualitative Examination." *Journal of Lesbian Studies* 3, no. 4 (1999): 27–36.

Textor, Alex. "Organization, Specialization, and Desires in the Big Men's Movement: Preliminary Research in the Study of Subculture-Formation." *International Journal of Sexuality and Gender Studies* 4, no. 3 (July 1999): 217–39.

Thomas, Carol. "Theorising Disability and Chronic Illness: Where Next for Perspectives in Medical Sociology?" *Social Theory & Health* 10, no. 3 (August 2012): 209–28.

Thomas, William, and Dorothy Thomas. *The Child in America: Behavior Problems and Programs*. New York: Knopf, 1928.

Turner, Victor. *Dramas, Fields, and Metaphors: Symbolic Action in Human Society*. Ithaca, N.Y.: Cornell University Press, 1974.

Van Iquity, Sister Dana. "Drags on Parade." *San Francisco Bay Times*, June 22, 2006, http://www.sfbaytimes.com/index.php?article_id=5300&sec=article. Accessed July 6, 2012.

Van Maanen, John. *Tales of the Field: On Writing Ethnography*. Chicago: University of Chicago Press, 1988.

Veblen, Thorstein. *The Theory of the Leisure Class*, 1899. Rockville, Md.: Arc Manor, 2008.

Walters, Suzanna. *All the Rage: The Story of Gay Visibility in America*. Chicago: University of Chicago Press, 2001.

Wann, Marilyn. "Taking the Waters." *Radiance: The Magazine for Large Women* 34 (April 1993): 40–45.

———. *Fat!So? Because You Don't Have to Apologize for Your Size!* Berkeley, Calif.: Ten Speed Press, 1998.

Weininger, Elliot. "Foundations of Pierre Bourdieu's Class Analysis." In *Approaches to Class Analysis*, edited by Erik Wright, 119–49. Cambridge: Cambridge University Press, 2005.

Whitesel, Jason. "Fatvertising: Refiguring Fat Gay Men in Cyberspace." *Limina: A Journal of Historical and Cultural Studies* 13 (2007): 92–102.

———. "Gay Men's Use of Online Pictures in Fat-Affirming Groups." In *LGBT Identity and Online New Media*, edited by Christopher Pullen and Margaret Cooper, 215–29. New York: Routledge, 2010.

Whitesel, Jason, and Amy Shuman. "Normalizing Desire: Stigma and the Carnivalesque in Gay Bigmen's Cultural Practices." *Men and Masculinities* 16, no. 4 (2013): 478–96.

Young, Katharine, ed. *Bodylore*. Knoxville: University of Tennessee Press, 1995.

INDEX

ABOUT THE AUTHOR

Jason Whitesel is Assistant Professor of Women's and Gender Studies at Pace University, New York.